Step By Step
Pre-empts

Alan Mould

B. T. Batsford Ltd, *London*

First published 1997

© Alan Mould 1997

ISBN 0 7134 8163 3

A CIP catalogue record for this book is available from the British Library.

Typeset by Apsbridge Services Ltd, Nottingham.
Printed by Redwood Books, Trowbridge, Wiltshire
for the publishers,
B. T. Batsford Ltd, 583 Fulham Road,
London SW6 5BY

A BATSFORD BRIDGE BOOK
Series Editor: Tony Sowter

CONTENTS

	Foreword	4
1	The Natural Three Level Pre-empt	5
2	Responding To Sound Three Level Pre-empts	25
3	Responding to Wild and Random Three Level Pre-empts	65
4	The Natural Weak Two Bid	95
5	Responding To Natural Weak Twos	115
6	Pre-empts in Competition	133

FOREWORD

This book is about natural pre-empts and how to respond to them. It is not about weird and wonderful artificial conventions. It is about opening pre-empts at the two, three and four level, when to open at what level and why. The book discusses in detail the various factors governing the choice such as vulnerability and table position. Crucially, the importance of partnership style on pre-emptive openings is examined in detail. Any partnership will achieve nothing but a long set of disastrous results unless its members have a common understanding of the kind of hands that are to be opened at each level. Only when this common understanding is achieved can any sensible approach to responding to partner's pre-empts happen.

You will find that at various points throughout the book I have used the same or very similar example hands. This is not laziness on my part for once. I wanted to show the dramatic effort that vulnerability, position at the table, and especially partnership style, can have on how to respond to a pre-empt. Put bluntly, you need very different types of hand to bid on, and have different aims in mind when you do, when partner's suit is king queen jack to seven compared with partner's suit of six small. I hope that by the end of this book you will know what partner will have and what to do with that knowledge.

The final chapter of the book deals with pre-empts in competitive situations and I advise a thorough reading of this. Nowhere has bidding improved so much in the last ten years than in modern players' ability to get into the opposition's auctions at a high level and make life awkward for them. But it is still little known outside expert circles. You will find that pre-empting in competitive situations improves your results out of all proportion to the effort you have to put in.

Alan Mould
April 1997

1
THE NATURAL THREE LEVEL PRE-EMPT

It's a funny old game football. And so for that matter is bridge. There are not that many games where you play to lose. Yet in a sense that is exactly what you are doing when you pre-empt. You are bidding a contract that you do not expect to make. So why? Because you are concerned that the opposition, left to their own devices, can bid to a much more lucrative contract. Hence you try to throw a spanner in the works. Thus, your assumption is that you are going to lose on this hand and you are simply attempting to minimise the loss. An odd situation for a game, but probably terribly good practice for life! So endeth the moral lecture.

Now, what sort of hands should we pre-empt on? Well, we all know the answer to that. We should have KQJ109xx and no other high cards at all. So that's solved that problem. Of course, the difficulty is that you pick this hand up once every two years and when you do that's fine. However, team-mates tend to get a bit depressed when they are consistently given a hard time by people opening at the three level and you keep on passing with the smug comment that 'I couldn't pre-empt because I didn't have the ♣10'. Like a lot of extreme positions, reserving your pre-empts for such 'pure' hands is theoretically unchallengeable and practically unworkable.

So, to repeat, what sort of hands should we pre-empt on? The 'established' rule for pre-empts is 'the rule of 500'. This states that your pre-empts should be going for 500 if doubled and partner puts down nothing of any value to you. So non-vulnerable you should have about six playing tricks for a pre-empt and vulnerable you should have about seven playing tricks. Thus:

> ♠ xx
> ♡ x
> ◊ xxx
> ♣ KQJ10xxx

is ideal non-vulnerable and:

♠ xx
♡ x
♢ xx
♣ KQJ10xxxx

is ideal vulnerable. This policy seems to give a sensible approach to pre-empts whilst not risking large penalties and hence might be seen as a sound approach to pre-empting.

However, almost nobody subscribes to this view any more. The tendency of modern players has been to devalue the requirements for a pre-empt more and more. Particularly in Britain, there is a school of players who seem to feel that a pre-empt is not a well considered tactical shot but merely an expression of machismo. If you haven't opened a pre-empt on jack to five and nothing else in the last six hands then you cannot call yourself a bridge player. For this school the rule of 500 becomes the rule of 800, 1100, 1400, they never double you anyway, and what's the odd 2000 between friends. This style of pre-empting has a number of adherents and I will examine the pros and cons later on.

So, the answer to the question of 'What sort of hands should we pre-empt on' is, 'It depends'. Depends on what? All sorts of things: vulnerability, position at the table, the opposition, your offence to defence ratio, and perhaps most important of all, partnership 'philosophy'. Let's deal with these one at a time.

Offence to Defence Ratio

Offence to defence ratio is an 'in' concept in bridge circles these days (or should it be bridge squares? Whoever heard of playing on a circular table?). The idea is simple enough. With all hands you should try and assess how much offence (ability to take tricks if you declare in your preferred trump suit) you have compared with how much defence (ability to take tricks if the opponents declare) you have. The greater the offence to defence ratio the more you should strive to declare; the lower the offence to defence ratio the more you should be happy to defend. We all do this unconsciously anyway but it is worthwhile thinking about it logically and consciously. It will often help us to make a sensible decision about when to pre-empt and when not to or when to defend and when to take a push.

What gives a high offence to defence ratio? Again we all know most of this intuitively but it is worth stating the various factors so that clear decisions can be made.

Firstly, the more distributional your hand is the higher the offensive potential. Thus you should be much more inclined to bid and pre-empt on highly distributional hands than on balanced or semi-balanced hands.

♠ KQJxxxx
♡ –
♢ KQxxx
♣ x

is a very powerful offensive hand with relatively little defence.

♠ KQJxxxx
♡ xx
♢ KQ
♣ xx

is much less powerful offensively but if anything has slightly more defence.

♠ KQJx
♡ xxx
♢ KQx
♣ xxx

is a very poor offensive hand but has considerable defensive potential.

Secondly, the honour structure is of vital importance here. Honours in long suits (particularly minor ones) add greatly to the offensive strength whereas honours in short suits add to the defensive strength. Thus:

♠ KQJxxxxx
♡ Axx
♢ xx
♣ –

is a highly offensive hand whereas:

♠ 109xxxxxx
♡ AQx
♢ KJ
♣ –

is much more defensive despite it having the same honour strength and distribution. The reason for this is obvious. With any suit other than spades as trumps the ♠KQJ in the first hand will never make tricks, whereas, the ♡Q and the ♢KJ in the second hand are quite likely to make tricks regardless of which suit are trumps. This is particularly the case if the opposition declare when they will not have the benefit of seeing one of your partnership's hands.

Thirdly the type of honours is important. Aces and kings are, in general, good for both offence and defence, but this is not so for queens and jacks. For offence you want queens and jacks in your long suits; they are often useless in your short suits. For defence you want queens and jacks in your short suits. You are not going to make the ♠J of your seven card suit if the opponents are playing in hearts; however, you are quite likely to make a trick from your ♢Jxx. Even if you do not, holdings such as these prevent partner's honours being finessed and hence increase the combined defensive potential of the hands. If you and your partner's combined diamond holding is xx opposite Qxx then declarer can always avoid a loser if s/he guesses correctly (and don't they always guess correctly against you?). However, if your combined defensive holding is Jx opposite Qxx then unless you kindly lead the suit for them declarer has to lose a trick in it. But that same Jx is likely to be useless to you on offence. You are still going to lose two tricks in the suit and the pitch on the queen will be of no value unless you have a loser elsewhere that cannot be attacked in time, which is relatively unlikely. So a stray jack can be a full trick in defence but useless in offence. This is worth bearing in mind!

Finally, the pips in your suits have an effect on the offence to defence ratio. This is what Andrew Robson refers to every chance he gets as 'impletion'. Again, basically, you want good pips in your long suits and not particularly in your short suits. KQ109876 is a much stronger suit that KQ65432. In the first case you cannot lose more than two tricks even opposite a void and if the jack drops you get out for one loser. In the second case, the very best you can hope for is two losers opposite a void or a singleton; no honours dropping are of any use to you since you hold no pips and if the suit breaks poorly you could lose four or even five tricks in it. On the other side, pips in your short suits often add to the defensive potential of the hand, not so much because they are tricks per se but because they prevent declarer having free finesses. If the defensive holding is Q8x opposite xx then declarer can finesse in either direction. However, if we change that to Q8x opposite 109 then declarer has only a one way finesse, either the queen is right or wrong and there is no choice in the matter.

A much overlooked area is that your offence to defence ratio often has effects on the bidding. The higher your defensive potential the lower the opposition are likely to bid! They will downgrade honours in your suits for offensive purposes; they will look worriedly at poor pips in their suits; they will be concerned about missing honours in their suits and/or relatively balanced hands. Moreover, if you have lots of stray honours lying around that are of no use to you they nevertheless reduce the overall point count that the opposition can have. This means that they simply may not have the values to bid.

All of this adds up to the fact that if you pre-empt on defence-rich hands you may be pre-empting the opposition out of a game they were not going to bid in the first place and which might not make even if they had! Not such a bright idea! However, on the other hand you may push them into a game they cannot make …. Which is why there are no perfect solutions. This is a good thing since, if there were, the game would have got very boring long ago.

So, what is the effect of all this waffle on pre-empts? Simply put, you should be more inclined to pre-empt and to pre-empt higher on offence rich hands and less inclined to pre-empt, or to pre-empt lower on defence rich hands. So:

♠ xxx
♡ x
◇ xx
♣ KQJ109xx

is the perfect pre-empt. Lloyds would underwrite you (not that that means much these days) to take 6 tricks with clubs as trumps and yet you would be lucky to take any tricks at all with anything else as trumps. On the other hand:

♠ K
♡ Qxx
◇ Jx
♣ K875432

is an awful pre-empt! If they double you, you are going for a fortune; you have stacks of defence (a potential trick in every suit) and a relatively high point count so the opposition might not have been bidding game even when they could make it! John Armstrong, one of the most aggressive/ wild/random/mad/successful (delete adjectives according to taste) pre-emptors around in Britain today once told me that in his experience outside queens are the worst thing to have in a pre-empt. As the opposition can see the position in the suit, hanging outside queens rarely make a trick on offence but they frequently make tricks in defence. When one of the most aggressive pre-emptors tells you he is loth to pre-empt with outside queens you should take notice.

Vulnerability

The effect of vulnerability is obvious. The more favourable the vulnerability to you the more aggressively you should pre-empt; the more unfavourable the less aggressively you should pre-empt. At Red (vulnerable versus non-vulnerable) your pre-empts should be very sound. You cannot be too careful. In a recent Camrose trial there was a flat board around the room where everybody first in hand at Red opened 3◇ on:

♠ Jx
♡ x
◇ AKJ98xxx
♣ xx

This went take out double, all pass and the result was -800 without the option. The defence could and did keep declarer off the table so he could not take the diamond finesse so he made just six trump tricks. Oh, by the way the opposition were lay down for 3NT for 400 and might be able to make 5♣ on a good day.

Don't forget also that they don't have to double you. If you go around opening 3◇ at Red on:

♠ xx
♡ xx
◇ K1085432
♣ Qx

because you want to show how macho you are; you're worried about your bald patch; your girl friend has just left you or for any other reason (I am suggesting here that most of the craziest pre-emptors are male) then, even if they pass you out, partner provides a couple of tricks and you go gently three off with the diamond finesse wrong, -300 is not a good board on what is likely to be a part score board. On the other hand, in a lot of partnerships that hand would be considered perfectly acceptable at Green (non-vulnerable versus vulnerable). Here, if you go three off undoubled -150 is OK if it is a part score board and three off doubled shows a profit if the opposition would have made game; even four off doubled is only a 5 IMP loss against a game.

Position at the Table

Position at the table is highly relevant to your pre-empts. First in hand your pre-empts should be up to whatever standard your partnership defines – more of that later. It is not generally appreciated however that your pre-empts should be sounder second in hand than first in hand. Why? Simply because one of the opponents has already passed. This has a number of negative effects on the usefulness of your pre-empt.

Firstly, it is as likely to be partner that you are pre-empting as the opposition. First in hand you have two opponents and only one partner (or three opponents in certain partnerships), so you are more likely to hit the opponents with the balance of the values. Second in hand when one opponent has already passed, it is as likely to be partner as LHO with the good hand.

Secondly, your opponents can use the pass to good use. Your LHO need not strain to bid on marginal hands as s/he may have felt it essential to do over a first in hand pre-empt since s/he knows that partner has not got very much. Your RHO can freely protect with a bid (or usually worst of all with a double) without fear of overstating their values since they have already passed.

Thirdly, pre-empts tend to be at their most effective when you hit the opposition with one of two types of hands. The first is two relatively balanced minimum opening strength hands. You can get pre-empts passed out on occasions when the opposition have a flat 13 count facing a flat 13 count and neither feels that they quite have the values to act. The second is a very good hand facing a decent but not exceptional hand. In this case both opponents tend to underbid a little to ensure the plus score. I once saw a flat board in a match between two teams of internationals as a result of a first in hand 3♠ on:

♠ 10xxxxxx
♡ 10xxx
◇ x
♣ x

(yes, they were at Green before you ask). At both tables the bidding continued 3NT, all pass. The 3NT was on a flat 25 count including ♠AKJx and the pass was on a flat 12 count including ♠Qx. Both declarers claimed 13 tricks at trick 1.

The point is that neither of these great results can happen if you are pre-empting second in hand. Both are excluded by the initial pass.

It is much easier for the opposition to sort out their combined assets after a second in hand pre-empt since they have the extra information that one of them has passed. Hence, second in hand pre-empts ought to be considerably sounder than first in hand pre-empts. There is less to gain and more to lose.

Third in hand pre-empts, as is well known, offer the greatest scope for the exercise of imagination, cunning, machismo or lunacy. Partner has passed so there is no danger of hitting partner with a good hand. So has RHO, so if you have a poor hand then LHO must have a good one and you might do some damage with a well aimed-blow. Thus at Green, most partnerships allow their third in hand pre-empts to be just about anything. For example:

♠ QJxxxx
♡ x
◇ Kxxx
♣ xx

would be perfectly acceptable for 3♠ in most partnerships. However, there is no reason why the third in hand pre-empt should always be weaker than normal; effective results can often be obtained by a stronger effort than standard. For example, a third in hand 3◇ on:

♠ x
♡ xx
◇ AKJ10xx
♣ AJxx

may be quite effective at keeping the opponents out of the majors whilst at the same time finding a making part score yourself. It is true that occasionally this may cause you to miss a game but this is really much less likely after partner has passed.

Fourth in hand pre-empts are quite the reverse side of the coin. Why are you trying to stop the opposition bidding to a lucrative contract when they were quite happy to pass the hand out? Logically fourth in hand pre-empts should be highly constructive. They should show specific types of hand pattern so that partner is able to judge accurately whether or not the partnership have a game on. The most sensible use for fourth in hand pre-empts at any vulnerability is to show a very good suit, at least KQJxxxx. Even if you regularly pre-empt on six card suits, fourth in hand pre-empts should guarantee seven as a minimum. Primarily the aim of the exercise is to encourage partner to bid 3NT if at all possible. So after:

```
Pass      Pass      Pass      3◇
Pass      ?
```

partner should be able to cheerfully bid 3NT on:

♠ Axx
♡ Axx
◇ Qx
♣ xxxxx

in the firm expectation of having at least nine tricks on top. Similarly, after:

```
Pass      Pass      Pass      3♠
Pass      ?
```

partner should be able to bid 4♠ on:

♠ Qxx
♡ xxxx
◇ AQJxx
♣ x

with hope of considerable play for game.

Tony Forrester in his book *Secrets of Success* has a cute idea about how to talk about the various strengths of pre-empts, so without more ado I shall steal it. His idea is that if you consider the 'perfect pre-empt' as:

♠ xx
♡ xx
◇ xx
♣ AKQxxxx

then that is awarded a score of 10. Any variation from this is then awarded an appropriately lower (or possibly higher score). So:

♠ xx
♡ xx
◇ xx
♣ Q10xxxxx

might be awarded 3 out of 10 and:

♠ xxx
♡ xx
◇ xx
♣ J98xxx

perhaps a generous 1. Tony then goes on to give what he refers to as a solid person's guide to the strength of pre-empts, varying from 10 out of 10 in any second or fourth position to 3 out of 10 third in hand at Green. Whilst I have no intention of providing such a doctrinal table (it is for individual partnerships to decide on the strength of their pre-empts) Tony's idea provides a sensible way for partnerships to discuss what might be the acceptable strength for a pre-empt at various vulnerabilities and position.

Partnership Philosophy

Without doubt, the single most important factor in determining the strength of your pre-empts is your partnership's philosophy on pre-emption and its temperament. Do you pride yourselves on the solidity of your game? Are you clear that you are never going to throw away a match? That the opponents are going to have to take it from you? Then stay away from wild or random pre-empts. Throw a few of those in and you will irritate partner and break partnership confidence, possibly forever. On the other hand, do you believe that it is a bidder's game? That you should go out there and make life as tough as possible for the opponents? Do you believe that you should force them to make decisions all the time? Is your partnership able and prepared to accept the odd -1100 with equanimity when the opponents were cold for 2♠? If so, then by all means go ahead and indulge yourselves in wild and random pre-empts. Do you believe in something in-between these two extremes? Perhaps being very sound vulnerable and very random non-vulnerable or being very sound everywhere except third in hand in which case partner has licence to do whatever they like? What matters far more than what you pre-empt on is what your partner will expect you to have for a pre-empt. If you consistently differ from partner's expectation then you are likely to end up with silly results in all directions; -800 in game and/or +170 with 6♦ cold.

One important area to discuss before the subject of suit quality even comes up is the number of cards in the suit partner can expect from a pre-empt in various positions. Twenty years ago, like so many other things in bridge, this simply would not have been an issue. Then, overcalls guaranteed five cards suits and usually six, you needed 26 points to make 3NT and pre-empts guaranteed seven card suits and quite likely eight if vulnerable. Forget such luxuries now. The exchange rate for cards to the pre-empt is spiralling down all the time. Non-vulnerable pre-empts are now commonly made in virtually any expert partnership on six card suits.

Some partnerships allow pre-empts (particularly third in hand) on five card suits. Why? Because experience has shown that they work. Yes, the absence of an extra card is of relevance on occasions. If you get doubled you have one less trump and therefore one more likely loser. Partner cannot bid game so freely depending on you for seven tricks. But that does not matter because most of the time you do not get doubled. Most of the time partner does not have a good hand. Most of the time opponents are capable of bidding to a reasonable contract left to themselves. Hence there is a considerable advantage in being able to open pre-empts with six card suits, simply because six card suits come up more often than seven card suits.

If you wish to open six card pre-empts and there is no doubt that they are big winners, then your partner has to be aware of this likelihood and compensate accordingly. It is no good partner gaily bidding 3NT on a couple of aces and a fitting honour if you are likely to put down KJxxxx and nothing else. Partner must be aware of this and, of course, so must the opponents. Your tendency to pre-empt on six card suits should clearly be stated on the convention card. Similarly, if you feel that it is tactically sensible to pre-empt on five card suits in certain situations, then it is essential that partner is on the same wavelength, otherwise nightmares will start occurring. For example I know a number of players who would consider a third in hand 3 ◇ at Green on:

♠ Qxx
♡ xx
◇ KQxxx
♣ xxx

as simply routine. Unless partner (and of course the opposition) are aware of this, all sorts of problems are likely to occur.

A similar problem concerns suit quality. How many honours and pips is partner entitled to expect in your suit when you pre-empt? A number of partnerships have a rule particularly about minor suit pre-empts that they should guarantee two of the top three honours. This is for the obvious reason that partner with the missing honour and a few bits can bid 3NT in the full expectation of being able to run your suit. Some partnerships have this rule in first or second position but not in third. Some have it only for minor suits but not for major ones. The problem is, of course, that this significantly limits the number of hands that you can pre-empt on. Playing in this way you have no choice but to pass with:

♠ xxx
♡ x
◇ xx
♣ AJ98765

regardless of the vulnerability, which may not strike you as a very sensible idea (it certainly doesn't to me). Moreover, you have to decide if a six card suit to two of the top three honours is acceptable or not. If partner bids 3NT on a couple of aces and Kx in your suit, that is fine if you are going to put down AQxxxxx, but not if you are going to put down AQJxxx. All of these issues have to be decided in any serious partnership if you want to make any profit at all out of your pre-empts or have any idea at all what is going on.

However, important as the above is, it is still all fine tuning. The central issue here is are your pre-empts basically sound, basically wild or simply random? I have touched on this in the above but let us look at it in a lot more detail. Each style has its firm adherents.

Solid Pre-emptive Style

Those who advocate a solid pre-emptive style point to all the advantages that accrue when a pre-empt is opened. It makes constructive bidding much easier (or as easy as it ever is when some buffoon opens a pre-empt). 3NT can be bid with confidence of what is in partner's hand. A solid pre-emptive style makes it easier both to sacrifice (since you know about how many tricks to expect from partner) and also to double the opposition when they step out of line (since you know about what to expect in the way of defence from partner). One of the English pairings, John Helme and Paul Bowyer, produce many +500s by insisting on sound pre-empts and then punishing opponents who bid over them at the wrong time.

Wild Pre-emptive Style

Those who advocate a wild pre-emptive style point out that most opposition these days are capable of bidding to a sensible contract left to themselves (and those that cannot one hopes to beat anyway). Therefore it is not enough to sit around waiting for good pre-empts; you need to get in and disrupt the opposition bidding on the slightest pretext. Yes, you go for a fortune occasionally but this is far outweighed by the damage you do to the opposition's constructive bidding by continually opening at the two, three or four level. The down side of this style (apart from the occasional 1100) is that partner must be much more circumspect in bidding over the pre-empt, both constructively and destructively.

The far end of the spectrum is to allow pre-empts, particularly first and third in hand at Green, on just about anything. One of the earliest exponents of these (there are now many others) in Britain were Graham Kirby and John Armstrong. One of their more noted examples occurred when John opened 3♣ second in hand at Green playing against Scotland in a Camrose match on:

♠ 543
♡ 652
◇ 84
♣ J7643

In this case he caught partner with a 3-5-5-0 shape and a 16 count. Graham passed 3♣ which drifted five down with an easy part score in hearts available (in fact the cards were lying so well that you could make 4♡). Were Kirby-Armstrong bothered about this? Not a bit of it. They simply shrugged their shoulders and went onto the next hand. They believed that on the whole these bids were winners and that was the end of it. They were not alone in this opinion. Tony Forrester wrote up this hand when he reported on the match. Since he was at the other table at the time one might suspect that he would not be very complimentary about losing 9 IMPs in such a fashion. However, his opinion was that, despite the result:

'These bids are big winners provided that:

> *(i) You have the bottle and,*
> *(ii) You have the temperament to accept the occasional silly result.*

Kirby-Armstrong have both.'

This is not the only view of such bids of course. A very well-known player commenting on this very hand wrote recently that opening 3♣ on the hand above was:

> *'extraordinary enough in itself, however what was even more remarkable was that he opened in front of his partner. James T. Kirk move over and let John sit down ....*
>
> *From his point of view this was all great fun, but his team-mates, amazingly enough, were slightly less amused. John would say that he*

is now ten years older. He would need at least the queen of clubs to make the bid.'

Who was this player who is so disparaging about John Armstrong's effort on the hand? Well, it is the same Tony Forrester actually, merely ten years older! So something has happened to Tony's views of pre-empts in that period. Maybe he has found that the random tactics do not work as well as he originally felt. Maybe they do not work so well against world class opposition. Maybe he feels his ability will carry him through and such tactics are not necessary to win. Maybe he is just getting older. Whatever the reason, it is clear that people's attitudes to pre-empts can change as time goes by and experience builds. It is also clear that people can have very clear and set ideas about the kind of hands that constitute a pre-empt and deviating from these can cause all sorts of problems to a partnership.

Lest you go around thinking that expert partnerships limit this sort of escapade to Green pre-empts, let me disabuse you. Some pairs simply have no fear! In the World Pairs final Jeff Meckstroth opened 2NT at Red. Eric Rodwell alerted and on enquiry explained that 2NT showed a bad pre-empt in an unspecified suit and that it could be 'very weak indeed'. This got the question 'What, even at this vulnerability?' – to which he replied 'Oh, we don't bother looking at the colour of the board!'. (Colour is an American term for vulnerability of the board.) Meckstroth's hand lived up (or down) to his partner's description since it was:

♠ xx
♡ Qx
◊ 10xxxxx
♣ xxx

This, vulnerable against not! Now Meckstroth-Rodwell are many people's choice for the world's best pair, so they must get good results with this kind of effort or they wouldn't do it. It is worth pointing out that in the year from which this hand is taken they went on to win the World Pairs by seven clear tops, the largest winning margin ever.

One of the difficulties of pre-empting on such very weak hands (apart from the necessity for strong nerve pills of course) is what do you do when you pick up a 'normal' pre-empt? That is, what do you do with KQJ to six or seven clubs at Green? If you open jack to five 3♣ and KQJ to seven 3♣ as well then you will certainly be pre-empting as often as possible but you will be causing huge headaches for your poor partner. Every time partner has some sort of flat 18 count with honour to three in your suit partner will not have the faintest idea what on earth to do. If they pass you can put down a good pre-empt and a cold game, or even a slam, will have been missed. If they bid 3NT or anything else, then they will be turning a plus score into a negative score when you have the real rubbish. They are three possible solutions to this.

One is to open the more normal pre-empts at one level higher, i.e. open sound players' three level pre-empts at the four level. You would probably be very surprised at what wild players will open on at the four level as a result of this style. Playing against me recently a wild pre-emptor opened 4♡ second in hand at Green on:

♠ xx
♡ QJ97xx
◇ –
♣ J10xxx

since he was too good for 3♡ in his style! Pass was, of course, never considered as an option. This is OK (provided your stomach can take it) if the suit is a major. It is more than a little silly however if the suit is a minor. If you have to open 4♣ (even assuming that the bid is available naturally; many pairs play 4♣/◇ as good 4♡/♠ bids), every time you pick up ♣KQJ to seven because you are too good for 3♣, then you have gone past the most likely game on the hand; to wit 3NT. Not a sensible idea.

The second possible solution is simply to pass 'normal' pre-empts, particularly not vulnerable, as they are too good in your style. I read a report of a recent American tournament where an international player passed:

♠ x
♡ xxx
◇ xxx
♣ KQJ10xx

first in hand at Green because he was too good to open 3♣ at that vulnerability in his style. This solution does have the major merit that at least now partner knows what is going on. You always have a complete load of rhubarb. The downside of this, of course, is that you do not get to pre-empt as often as you might and you do not get to pre-empt on hands that normal players would and hence you are 'playing against' everyone else. It certainly does not look sensible bridge to me to pass this hand and it causes me no pain to report that the decision worked very badly.

The third possible solution is simply to go ahead and open all the hands, good, bad and ugly, with the same pre-emptive call and damn the consequences. In the terminology I am using in this book you are then no longer really playing wild pre-empts. You are playing random pre-empts.

Random Pre-emptive Style

A random pre-emptive style is where you believe it is of value to pre-empt on many different types of hand with the same bid. The late Terence Reese was a firm advocate of this (though he always vilified the modern practice of hyper-light pre-empts) and frequently quoted that 'a pre-empt that is known to be always weak is a blunt tool'. He was particularly in favour of pre-empting on quite strong hands in various circumstances. One of the most spectacular successes of this I ever saw was produced by Howard Melbourne, a player noted for his imagination. In a Gold Cup match many years ago Rob Sheehan passed as dealer with:

♠ 52
♡ Q765432
◇ AQ5
♣ Q

since no opening bid seemed to be sensible. The bidding now proceeded in tempo 3♠ from Howard on his left, pass, pass to him. He decided to protect with 4♡. This drew a double from Howard and everybody passed. Dummy produced a flat two count! Rob asked Howard's partner at this point if they played 'normal' pre-empts. Howard's partner gave quite a good answer, I thought, when he said 'That doesn't sound like one!'. He was certainly right since Howard's hand for a second in hand 3♠ was:

♠ AKJ103
♡ AJ108
◇ 7
♣ A107!

Now, I am hardly advocating this as sound but it just shows what can happen if you vary the strength of your pre-empts.

Real flights of fancy such as that one by Howard aside, what I really mean by a random pre-emptive style is that three level pre-empts can show anything from a sound pre-empt to as wild a pre-empt as your partnership will allow. So non-vulnerable, and particularly at Green, the suit could vary from KJ to seven, through KQJ to six, to 10 to six and on to KQ to five if that is your bottom limit. Vulnerable the suit could be anything from AKJ to seven down to KQ10 to six if that is your lower limit.

As I said, in this style, you get to pre-empt as often as possible and the opposition are completely in the dark about your hand type. The problem is that so is partner. Every time partner has a good hand it is a complete guess for them whether they should move or not. But the advocates of this style argue that that is a price worth paying for the extra grief caused the opponents by pre-empting as often as possible. There are after all two opponents to confuse and only one partner, they argue. If this style attracts you try it out. But I warn you it is not easy to play. Be prepared for some very silly results in all directions. You will have some ridiculously bad results to go with your very good ones. Random bids tend to yield random results.

Four Level Opening Bids

I am going to assume here that all your four level opening bids are natural, particularly 4♣/4♢ are natural rather than conventional. On what type of hand should you open a four level pre-empt rather than a three level pre-empt? The simple answer to that is a better one, i.e. a hand with more offence in it. So essentially you want about a trick more than you would be prepared to open at the three level. This means that all the factors we have discussed already in relation to pre-empts, offence to defence ratio, vulnerability, position at the table, pre-emptive style, etc., come into play. Of particular relevance in four level opening bids, especially four of a major, is a high offensive ratio. The reason for this is that you will nearly always end up playing the hand, undoubled if partner has a good hand and doubled if partner has a poor hand. It is relatively rare, though not of course impossible, for the opposition to bid over an opening four of a major since they will have to go to the five level (except 4♠ over 4♡). This means that when you open a four level pre-empt you must be prepared to play there. If you look at a hand and think 'Well, I'm going to open 4♠ but I hope they bid over it because I don't want to play in it doubled', then don't open it. A huge proportion of the time they will not bid over it. The opposition usually bid over three level pre-empts when they have the balance of power, but rarely over four level pre-empts.

So a high offensive ratio is necessary and distribution is a major factor in this. Let's assume for the moment that you are playing a sound pre-emptive style. Then first in hand non-vulnerable a 3 ♠ call might well look like:

♠ KQJxxx
♡ x
♢ xxx
♣ xxx

Yes, that is considered sound these days. No one can fault you for opening 3 ♠ on:

♠ KQJxxxx
♡ xx
♢ xx
♣ xx

You have a good seven card suit but the 'death pattern'. 7-2-2-2 patterns play very badly since partner needs so many high cards to cover all your losers. On the other hand it is positively wet to open 3 ♠ on:

♠ KQJxxxx
♡ –
♢ xxxx
♣ xx

Open 4 ♠. Here you have the same seven card suit but much better distribution plus a real worry about the heart suit. 4 ♠ cuts out the entire four level and is relatively safe. At worst you should get out for -800 which is not so bad against game. If partner is kind enough to put down something useful such as ♢ KQxx and nothing for example then you might be out for -100. Opposite the previous example you would still be going for -500.

Vulnerable four level pre-empts obviously have to be rather more circumspect. In a sound style, particularly at Red, the old rule of at least eight tricks is a very sensible one to follow. So a reasonable vulnerable 4 ♠ opener might be:

♠ AKJxxxxx
♡ x
♢ Kxx
♣ x

and a reasonable 4◊ opening might look like:

♠ –
♡ x
◊ KQJ10xxxx
♣ Kxxx

This does go past 3NT but it is much too strong for 3◊ even at Red. In addition with these majors you really want to try and keep them out as much as possible. In a sound style 5◊ is just too much though. It looks a very likely -800.

Four of a minor opening bids are reasonably well defined since they show hands with more offence that three of a minor, but not enough offence for five of a minor. By their nature, since they are game, four of a major openings carry a greater range than other pre-empts. 4♡ and 4♠ can vary from stretches non-vulnerable to quite hefty hands where you expect to make the contract but do not feel that you can investigate a slam sensibly. Curiously, vulnerable you may want to pre-empt on such hands not so much to prevent the opponents finding a making game but to prevent them finding a paying save. So vulnerable, 4♡ would be very sensible on:

♠ x
♡ KQJxxxxx
◊ KQJx
♣ –

where we certainly expect to make the contract but need two out of three aces from partner to make a slam. We also would prefer the opposition not to be able to find 4♠ or 5♣ against which we have zero defence. The best way of doing this is to open as high as possible as fast as possible, in this case 4♡. Similarly 4♠ is very sensible on:

♠ AQJxxxx
♡ –
◊ x
♣ Kxxxx

Here you know you want to play 4♠ and do not want the opposition in a Red suit. Get to 4♠ as fast as possible.

You can take things too far though. A pre-emptive opening on a hand such as:

♠ KQJxxxxx
♡ –
◇ AKQx
♣ x

even at Red is just silly. Here either black ace will make you virtually laydown for 6♠ and yet partner will not even think of moving with both black aces. Partners rarely move over a 4♡/4♠ opening since it carries such a wide range and they do not wish to jeopardise the plus score. And quite right too. In particular they always need good controls to go on. This means they will never go on if you have a fist full of controls and you will miss some slams opening hands like this four of a major. Many pairs have a rule that there must be no more than one first round control outside the trump suit and that seems a sensible idea to me. People who go around opening at the four level with a couple of outside aces must expect to play grand slams in game.

Finally, before we move on, what does a four level opening in a wild pre-emptive style look like? Well, you have already seen a shining example of one earlier in the chapter. Basically it looks like one trick more than a wild three bid and so it is whatever your partnership decides on as the bottom limit. In a wild style at Green there is no doubt that:

♠ KQJxxxx
♡ x
◇ xxx
♣ xx

would be opened 4♠ as would:

♠ QJ10xxx
♡ –
◇ KQxxx
♣ xx

You can immediately begin to see how much you need to move towards a slam opposite a wild four level opening.

2
RESPONDING TO SOUND THREE LEVEL PRE-EMPTS

Responding to pre-empts is the most difficult area of dealing with pre-empts. This surely is no surprise to us. Pre-empts are designed to make constructive bidding difficult by taking away as much bidding space as possible. If it is our side that is supposed to be bidding constructively then the loss of bidding space is just as much of a pain for us as for the opposition. To open a pre-empt is to play the percentages. You are gambling that it is their hand and not yours. The odds for this are in your favour since there are two opponents and only one partner (or friendly opponent as s/he is sometimes called) and you have a poor hand.

Well, how should you respond to pre-empts then? We can only answer this if we know what kind of pre-empts we are playing, sound, wild or random. It is impossible to bid sensibly over a pre-empt unless you know what the bid shows. I will thus examine each of the styles in turn and develop methods of responding to pre-empts.

It is only fair by now to tell you that by nature I am a sound pre-emptor. Yes, I open six card suits non-vulnerable, but so does everybody else, believe me. However, vulnerable I will always have seven card suits. I also do not go in for ten to six or queen to five openings at any vulnerability. My hair is white enough already and my card play isn't good enough. That is not to say that wild pre-empts cannot be very successful or that it may not be the correct way to play the game. They are just not for me. Right, having said that I will examine responding to each style in turn starting with sound pre-empts.

Responding to Sound Pre-empts

The traditional method and still the most widely used is that direct raises are pre-emptive, 3NT is to play and new suits are forcing for one round. The first two of these are self explanatory.

You should bid 3NT over a pre-empt every time you think you can make it. So assuming that you are playing sound pre-empts what would you bid of each of the following hands in response to 3♣?

(a)
    ♠ Axx
    ♡ KQxxx
    ◊ Ax
    ♣ Axx

(b)
    ♠ Axx
    ♡ Kx
    ◊ AKQJxxx
    ♣ x

(c)
    ♠ KQx
    ♡ AQxx
    ◊ AKJx
    ♣ Jx

(a) Answer: 3NT

You expect partner to have the ♣K so you can count seven club tricks and two aces as a minimum. If for some reason partner does not have the ♣K but a holding such as ♣QJ109xxx then you may survive anyway as partner may have an honour card to bolster your holding in the suit they lead. It is possible to construct hands where 4♡ is a better contract than 3NT but it would be quite wrong to introduce hearts at this point. Far and away the most likely game to make is 3NT so (to follow Hamman's rule) you should just bid it. Introducing hearts on this hand will just result in partner raising hearts on inadequate support or bidding 4♣ so bypassing 3NT. After all do you really expect partner to bid 3NT? That's your job and you should do it.

(b) Answer: 3NT

On this hand you hope for a heart lead at which point you can claim nine tricks opposite any 13 cards partner puts down. If the opposition are unkind enough to lead something else then you will have to try and find a trick from somewhere but that doesn't seem impossible. Anyway, as before, 3NT is the most likely game so you should simply bid it.

(c) Answer: 5♣

Hand (c) is not a 3NT bid. Despite having the highest point count of all the hands and a probable double stopper in every suit 3NT is not the right bid here. The problem is that you may very well never see dummy since you have no sure way of running the club suit. It is also difficult to see how you will come to nine tricks without the aid of partner's suit.

If partner, for example, tables a perfectly sensible:

♠ xxx
♡ x
♢ xx
♣ KQ98754

then you need stiff ♣A to make the contract and will go about three off if that does not happen. Partner will then enquire why this happened when this fine club suit is put down. And partner will be right. True 3NT need not be this bad. Change partner's clubs to AQ to seven for example and game is now on a finesse. Leave partner's clubs alone but give the hand an entry such as ♢Q or ♡K or even sometimes ♠J and 3NT is now excellent.

However, you need not take these risks, since you have a perfectly sound alternative. What is wrong with 5♣? On the example hand above 5♣ is cold if the spade finesse works and you can try ruffing out the ♢Q before falling back on that. Add the ♠J and 5♣ is cold with 3NT still not on the card. If partner has ♣AQ to seven then 5♣ will make every time 3NT does and will certainly go less off when neither makes.

Think about this. Give partner any hand where 3NT is good and you will find that 5♣ is just as good if not better. This might be more of a problem at Pairs where you may feel that you have to bid 3NT and hope for a good hand from partner but at Teams this is not a problem. Bid 5♣ and expect to make a comfortable eleven tricks. Contrast this approach with what to do opposite a wild pre-empt later on.

You can often get away with 3NT on somewhat less than ideal hands provided you have top tricks to run. For example, over 3♣ there is a lot to be said for 3NT on:

♠ Axx
♡ Axxx
◇ xxx
♣ Kxx

provided you are playing with a sound pre-emptor. This is hardly copper
bottomed with a completely unprotected suit but I would certainly bid it
vulnerable since a decent suit is expected for a vulnerable pre-empt.
Actually, I held this hand at the table after 3♣, doubled (takeout) and bid
3NT. I got a heart lead and partner tabled:

♠ Kxx
♡ xx
◇ x
♣ AJxxxxx

Ten rapid tricks later we moved on to the next hand. Yes, of course, they
could have taken five diamond tricks off the top but they didn't. Both the
opposition actions were perfectly sensible. RHO's take out double was on
a 4-3-5-1 shape and LHO had led the stronger of their four card suits.
Luckily for me this was hearts. But surely you would be happy to bid 3NT
that only depended on a blind lead by the opposition? I know I would. It
might also have been cold. Swap partner's Red suits and we need
diamonds 4-4; swap spades and diamonds and you need a lead from a high
doubleton diamond to beat the contract – hardly likely. But note that such
bids are only possible if you have a sound pre-emptive style. If partner is
liable to put down ♣QJxxxx and nothing else then 3NT is clearly absurd.

3NT used to be very popular as an out and out psyche as well on hands
such as:

♠ Axxx
♡ xx
◇ xxx
♣ Kxxx

or even:

♠ xxxx
♡ xx
◇ xxxx
♣ AKx

My feeling is that you need very naive opponents before you can get away with this kind of thing these days. Everybody has seen it too often before. These days fourth in hand tends to double with a decent hand or cuebids partner's suit with a distributional one. Effectively this means that you are giving them extra room and bids to sort out their hands. Not so clever now, are we? Usually you are much better off simply increasing the pre-empt and letting them sort it out rather than trying cute 3NT calls. That is not to say that you should never do it or that it never works. Occasionally you find a combination of the opponents' cards where they cannot pick up the psyche and you go gently six off undoubled. Occasionally you get doubled when you were genuine and make a comfortable overtrick. As the poker player said, sometimes you have to be caught bluffing, otherwise nobody will ever try and catch you bluffing. All I'm saying is that it is silly to try this regularly since it does give them more room when they pick it up and they will pick it up almost all of the time.

The upshot of all this is that the pre-emptor must pass 3NT regardless of what hand they have pre-empted on. I have frequently seen auctions such as:

3♣	Pass	3NT	Pass
4♣			

with the explanation that 'I had such a bad pre-empt, partner'. So flipping what? It is not any of your business once partner has bid 3NT. You get your dummy on the table and let partner get on with it. It does not matter if you play that pre-empts guarantee two of the top three honours and you have decided to try one on QJ10xxxx. It does not matter if you play sound pre-empts and you have decided the time has come to try one on Kxxxxx. Get your dummy down. Partner may have sufficient honours in your suit to run it anyway; partner may have a flat 22 count and just be able to make nine tricks in power; partner may have nine tricks in their own hand. In none of these cases is partner going to be enamoured by a 4♣ call from you. So don't do it.

It is clearly sensible to play that direct raises are pre-emptive, so upping the ante even more and making it steadily more difficult for the opposition to have any meaningful auction. The subject of just how high to raise partner though is hotly contested, with different camps as usual. Often, tactical considerations are present as well and many experts will bid different things on the same hand at different times to ensure the opposition are unsure of the position. This is an extension of the Reese principle. If the opponents know that you always bid to the maximum on any fit with partner and will always strain to raise the pre-empt on any poor hand, then they double you or bid on in the knowledge that their partner must have a reasonable hand. If, on the other hand, you sometimes raise on hands with some defence or sometimes do not raise on worthless hands then some doubt and insecurity is generated, which can only be to your advantage.

Let's look at some examples. On all occasions partner has opened 3♣ first in hand in a sound style and it goes pass on your right. What do you do with:

(a)	♠ xxxx ♡ x ◇ Axxxx ♣ Kxx		**(d)**	♠ xxx ♡ xxxx ◇ xxx ♣ Qxx
(b)	♠ xx ♡ x ◇ Qxxxxx ♣ Kxxx		**(e)**	♠ Ax ♡ xxx ◇ 10xxxxx ♣ QJ
(c)	♠ xxx ♡ xx ◇ Axxxx ♣ Kxx		**(f)**	♠ KJxx ♡ AQx ◇ Q10xx ♣ J10

Answers: Refuse to answer: 10 points each
              All other answers: 0 points each

How many did I get here? How can you possibly answer what you would bid if I do not tell you what the vulnerability is? In most cases you are deciding whether or not to sacrifice. It makes a massive difference if you are at Green or at Red. So let's try again. We will assume that you are at Green (i.e. not vulnerable against vulnerable opponents).

(a)   ♠ xxxx
                                ♡ x
                                ◇ Axxxx
                                ♣ Kxx

Answer: 5♣

This one seems fairly clear cut. You certainly expect the opposition to make 4♡. They seem to have at least nine hearts between them (unless partner has an unlikely four) and also plenty of high cards. There does not seem any way you can beat this except finding partner with a singleton diamond on the go and the ♣A. Moreover 5♣ looks to you to be very cheap. Unless you are very unlucky partner will have two or three hearts so you should have a ruff or two in your hand. If partner has ♣A to seven that will bring the total up to nine or ten. On a really good day you might even make this! Once in a blue moon partner has:

♠ x
♡ xxx
◇ Kx
♣ AJ9xxxx

and 5♣ (usually doubled) gets on the card. Okay, so this is an exceptionally good hand for a Green pre-empt but sometimes that's what you pick up. So go ahead and bid 5♣ and let the opposition sort it out. If they bid at the five level let them get on with it. It is true that you may well still be cheap in 6♣ but it is also true that you may beat a five level contract. The oft quoted rule that the five level belongs to the opposition should almost always be adhered to. If the opposition volunteer to try and take as many as 11 tricks, let them get on with it and see if they can.

(b)

♠ xx
♡ x
◇ Q98xxx
♣ Kxxx

Answer: 5♣

Again, you are certain that the opposition are cold for game and that 5♣ is going to be cheap, so why not go ahead and bid it? Well, there is a reason actually. Last time all you were worried about was the opposition's game. You had an ace and only three card support for partner. Here you are concerned that the opposition may be cold for rather more than game. A small slam is a definite possibility looking at your hand and partner's pre-empt and it would not surprise you if I told you they could make a grand slam. For this reason something other than 5♣ should be considered. Many players, and particularly the more aggressive ones would bid 6♣ on hand (b), reasoning that this will still be a reasonable save against game if that is all the opposition can make and it will make it almost impossible for the opposition to bid a slam. This is certainly true. If you bid 6♣ you must be sure that the opposition will not settle at the five level if you give them the chance. You will be almost certain to be doubled in 6♣, so you need to be sure that this is actually what you want to happen. But it is also true that a lot of the time you will be doubled in 5♣ as well, so why chuck away an extra 200 points (or possibly 300 these days)? Occasionally also this method backfires in that it can force a winning decision on a player who would not otherwise have made it. You may catch someone with ♡AK to eight and a couple of outside aces who simply feels constrained to shut their eyes and bid 6♡. Not what you want on this hand.

The opposite approach, which can be remarkably effective on many occasions is to 'under pre-empt'. So on this hand you could try 4♣. The idea here is twofold. Firstly if you pre-empt to the five or six level a player with say ♣xxx or even ♣xx can 'read' their partner's shortage and bid accordingly, 'knowing' that there is at most one club loser. So under pre-empting can disguise the extent of your fit and the opponents' are not so secure of their fit and shortages. Secondly you can give them enough rope to hang themselves with. On a number of occasions I have seen grand slams played in game after sequences such as:

3♣	Pass	4♣	4♡
All pass			

The reason for this is that, quite rightly, partnerships lay enormous stress on getting plus scores after the opposition pre-empt and in particular on securing the game bonus. So a player with a very good hand may well just bid game after:

3♣	Pass	4♣

in case partner has nothing. Similarly, a player who has heard the auction:

3♣	Pass	4♣	4♡
Pass			

will pass quite good hands for fear that his partner has (quite rightly) bid on a decent suit and little else. Take my example above. A player with ♡AK to eight and a couple of aces may feel constrained to bid 6♡ after:

3♣	Pass	6♣	??

That same player will certainly bid 5♡ after:

3♣	Pass	5♣	??

and may well be raised to 6♡ on general values by, say, a flat 13 count (particularly if extreme ♣ shortage can be read).

But that same player may well choose to only bid 4♡ after:

3♣   Pass   4♣   ??

and the flat 13 count opposite will now pass for sure. You may call 4♡ lily-livered but you would say it was well judged if partner put down a flat 5 or 6 count with no tricks and 4♡ just made.

The point is that if you always bid 5♣ or 6♣ on big fits then the opposition can never have this kind of 'disaster'. Nor am I advocating that you go around raising 3♣ to 4♣ every time you have a five card fit! What I am suggesting is that the power of raising to exactly four of a minor is rarely appreciated and you should bring it into your thinking more often. Giving the opposition to chance to subside in game when you think they have a slam on is.often worth a try. Also what I do advocate is that you do not do the same thing every time. On hand (b) most of the time I would bid 5♣ since I consider this to be a middle of the road, moderately conservative call. Sometimes though I will venture 6♣ and perhaps a little more often I might try 4♣. Your job in raising partner's pre-empt is to make life as difficult as possible for the opposition. If you always have exactly the same type of hand for your actions you are painting pretty pictures for them, not hindering them.

(c)   ♠ xxx
                                        ♡ xx
                                        ◇ Axxxx
                                        ♣ Kxx

Answer: ?

Who knows? This really does depend on just how sound your sound pre-empts are. You still feel that the opponents are very likely to have a game cold and 5♣ still appears to be a decent sacrifice so why do we not go ahead and bid it? It is after all the pressure bid which forces the opposition to make a decision at the five level. The problem with this approach is that they do not really have a decision. They will almost always double you and leave it at that. They are very unlikely to have more than a nine-card fit and possibly only an eight card fit so they are unlikely to have sufficient distribution to try a five level contract. Moreover, if partner has a good seven card suit such as ♣AQxxxxx you are not going to make more than 8 tricks unless partner has a slightly unlikely three hearts as well. -500 is not a marvellous save against a vulnerable game (3 IMPs). If partner is allowed to hold a six card suit (certainly my definition of a 'sound' Green pre-empt would include ♣AQJxxx for example) then it is quite likely that you will go for 800 against their game, which is now a loss of 5 IMPs. On a really 'good' day you will go for -800 when the opponents could not make game! Give partner a singleton diamond and ♣AQJxxx for example and ♢A will beat a major suit game on the go and a club lead will still beat it if the clubs are 2-2. That is then a really wonderful result, turning +100 into -800!

What then do I suggest you try with hand (c)? Well again I think it pays to mix it up a little. Go ahead and try 5♣ if you think it is right tactically and particularly do so against opposition who you think are likely to bid over it (or for that matter pass you out: it does still happen occasionally). The under pre-empt of pass is quite a good idea and would probably be my choice. You sometimes may get a protection from LHO on quite a reasonable hand and a pass from RHO on another quite reasonable hand, each underbidding slightly to try and get the plus score. This is an extension of the principle of allowing them to play at the four level above. This time you allow them to play at the three level; a longer piece of rope as it were. Certainly also 4♣ is a sensible call. This gives them the chance to double you and you don't particularly mind if they do since anything worse than -300 seems remote and it may be better than that. The real downside of 4♣ is that it will often force them into four of a major that they would not otherwise have bid. If they do this then it is likely to be correct, since your hand is so balanced that it will probably make even when it is not a very good contract.

(d)

> ♠ xxx
> ♡ xxxx
> ♢ xxx
> ♣ Qxx

Answer: ?

So what do you fancy on this one? The opposition are almost guaranteed to make a slam, so 5♣? 6♣? 7♣? In my opinion all of these are foolish, particularly 6♣ and 7♣. You are going for a fortune since the only possible tricks are in partner's hand. For example, give partner ♣AJ10xxxx and unless the stiff ♣K drops partner is going to make exactly six tricks. This is -1400 in 6♣ and -1700 in 7♣. -1400 is exactly +1 IMP if your team-mates manage to bid this slam and -1700 is -7 IMPs.

Notice that the opposition do not have to do anything clever here. They do not have to bid and make a slam, difficult enough at the best of times, trebly difficult when the bidding starts at the three level. All they have to do is say double with three quarters of the high cards in the pack between them, a feat usually within most pairs' ability. Worse, what if partner has ♣AKJ10xx? An eminently sound pre-empt and now the opposition cannot make a slam if the clubs are 2-2. Partner might have the ♣A and a stray king which makes a trick in defence or a stray queen that the opposition mis-guess the whereabouts of. So, in my opinion, 7♣, 6♣, and even 5♣ is giving the opposition fielder's choice. They will almost certainly choose to double you for well above the value of any game, so your team-mates will have to bid a slam to salvage anything. If the opposition do choose to bid on to a slam they will be doing so in the teeth of your pre-empt and will generally know what they are going.

What then do I suggest? A widely held view is 'Pass, and let them get on with it'. This view has much to commend it. If you do not tell them you have a club fit they will not know it and hence may grind to a halt worried about club wastage. As before 4♣ also has a lot to recommend it. The opposition may come to rest in four of a major if you let them and at least if they double you in 4♣ it will not be too expensive. The point is that, if the opposition are going to bid a slam, there is nothing that you can do about it. Your save is going to be much too expensive and any high level adventure will simply give an easier alternative to a four figure score.

(e)
        ♠ Ax
        ♡ xxx
        ◇ 1087xxx
        ♣ QJ

Answer: Pass

What do you fancy on (e)? Pass seems fair enough. You do not have great support for partner but neither do you expect them to make a slam so why not just pass and let the opposition decide what to do? On the other hand how about 4♣? You do after all expect the opposition to make four of a major so why not make it a bit tougher for them? Personally I do not mind this provided that (a) you are definitely playing sound pre-empts, (b) partner is not the type to bid again and (c) you accept that sometimes you will push them into a game that they would not otherwise have bid. This hand came up at the table and I'll tell you what happened to it later.

(f)   ♠ KJxx
                                 ♡ AQx
                                 ◊ Q10xx
                                 ♣ J10

Answer: Pass

Now, how about hand (f)? Isn't pass completely obvious? You have no
game ambition yourself and good defence to anything the opposition care
to bid. You certainly are very happy for them to bid a major so what's
wrong with pass? Well nothing at all, pass is clearly the sensible action
and I would choose it nine times out of ten. But it is not the only option
and it was not the one chosen at the table. The hand was held by, sadly, the
recently deceased Irving Rose who chose 4♣. This may seem mad but
think of the effect on your LHO. Both of you have advertised weakness.
Your LHO is under considerable pressure to bid since otherwise they
could be passing you out in 4♣ with game cold their way. Irving's gambit
caught a perfect hand for him on his left, a 13 count with ♡KJxxxx.
Everybody I know would bid 4♡ on this and so did the player at the table.
Irving doubled this on the return and generated +500 out of nowhere.

Now I'm not suggesting this is sound, nor even that it is the right tactic.
But it is worth trying sometimes. If it goes double all pass you will have
to hope for a sympathetic partner and team-mates as it will be a very silly
result. But sometimes, as for Irving here, it can generate a spectacularly
successful result. It has upsides in other ways as well. Sometimes you may
find that you get 4♣ passed out (doubled or not) when you have bid it with
(c) or (e) for fear that you may have hand (f) instead and that will show a
tidy profit. Notice how many hands I have suggested 4♣ as a possible bid:
five hands out of six ranging from hands with plenty of offence and no
defence against a slam to hands with good defence against game. If the
opponents know you only bid 4♣ on bad hands or only try to fool them
with 4♣ on good hands you will be very easy to play against. Mix it up
and you become a nightmare.

We move on at last to new suits. Traditionally, new suits (other than game
bids) have been treated as forcing so as to allow some development of the
hand. Typically then they will be bid on two types of good hand:

(i)   Hands with a fairly good major that is hoping for support
(ii) Hands which lack a stop for 3NT

Thus, for example, if we start with our ubiquitous 3♣ at Green in a sound style then let's look a few possible hands.

(a)	♠ AKx ♡ KQJxxx ◊ xx ♣ Ax	**(e)**	♠ AKxx ♡ xx ◊ AQxx ♣ AJx
(b)	♠ AK ♡ AKQJxxxx ◊ xx ♣ A	**(f)**	♠ AKxx ♡ AQx ◊ xx ♣ AJxx
(c)	♠ KQJxxx ♡ AKQxx ◊ xx ♣ −	**(g)**	♠ AQJx ♡ xxx ◊ xx ♣ Qxxx
(d)	♠ AJ10xxxx ♡ x ◊ Axx ♣ xx	**(h)**	♠ Axxx ♡ xx ◊ xxx ♣ Kxxx

(a)
          ♠ AKx
          ♡ KQJxxx
          ◊ xx
          ♣ Ax

Answer: 3♡

By bidding at all, we could be turning a plus score into a minus score. Nevertheless partner needs very little to make 4♡ so we have to give it a go. Moreover, 3NT could also be cold and we can explore that possibility by bidding 3♡ as well. Any genuine suit bid over a pre-empt (see below for examples of when to introduce a non-genuine suit) should be a decent six card suit at least. It is true that sometimes you can make game in a five three major suit fit after a pre-empt. But it is just too dangerous and puts too much strain on the bidding to go around trying to find such fits. Most of the time (particularly if your pre-empts are seven cards) partner will not have three cards in a major and even less often four cards. Thus, when you introduce a new suit, particularly a major, it should be a decent suit for which you are looking for tertiary support. Partner should look very favourably on honour one in your suit and be delighted with three small. It should be acceptable to raise on xx and you should be aware of this and be prepared for it. Yes you miss the odd five three fit but you get to all the 6-2 fits and that is really a lot more likely after a pre-empt.

(b)
♠ AK
♡ AKQJxxxx
♢ xx
♣ A

Answer: 3♡

Here you have a huge hand. Eleven tricks guaranteed in your own hand. It is perhaps not very likely but you could be cold for a slam, even a grand slam. Stranger things have happened than partner holding three low hearts and a void diamond for example. Your duty is to try and explore this option sensibly. So start with a forcing 3♡. If partner happens to support, great. You can continue with a 4♠ cuebid. If partner bids 3NT or 4♣, as is most likely then you are going to have to invent something. 4♠ is fine provided partner does not think you have a two suiter and tables the dummy. Otherwise you will probably have to try 5♡ and hope partner can work out that, if you were worried about spades, you could have tried 4♢ to be going on with. It is not easy but then some idiot has pre-empted, remember!

(c)
♠ KQJxxx
♡ AKQxx
♢ xx
♣ –

Answer: 3♠

If partner supports them you are delighted, otherwise you can continue with 4♡ and let partner choose. Again this is not copper-bottomed and you may well go off in game but there is just too much chance of game for you not to give it a try. A further incentive on this hand is that 3♣ could well be going off with four of a major making. A perfectly sensible hand from partner such as:

♠ x
♡ Jxx
♢ xx
♣ AQxxxxx

gives 3♣ no genuine play at all while 4♡ is excellent.

(d)   ♠ AJ10xxxx
                                     ♡ x
                                     ◇ Axx
                                     ♣ xx

Answer: 3♠

This has two advantages. It is possible that you can make 4♠ with some support from partner. Secondly the opposition are not dead yet. It is entirely possible that they have a heart contract on, and they could well make game in hearts. It is likely they will find their right level if left to themselves with a timid pass. Bidding 3♠ will help to keep them out and if it does not, then partner may be able to bid 4♠ or at least will know the best suit to lead. If all partner can do over 3♠ is bid 4♣, then you have to put down your dummy and accept what is almost certain to be a negative score. I know players who would have a go at 4♠ over 3♣ but, personally, I think this is unnecessarily aggressive. If 4♠ is going to make, partner will bid it over 3♠; if not, then why bid it?

(e)   ♠ AKxx
                                     ♡ xx
                                     ◇ AQxx
                                     ♣ AJx

Answer: 3◇

Here you are not interested in support and if partner is unkind enough to support you then you will retire back to partner's suit. In this case we are bidding 3◇ in the hope that partner has a heart stop in which case 3NT will be laydown. Partner will tell us if s/he has one (by bidding 3♡) and if not you can bid 5♣ in the sure knowledge that it is a decent contract. Indeed, sometimes you might be able to get to a cold slam facing, for example:

                                     ♠ xxx
                                     ♡ x
                                     ◇ Kx
                                     ♣ K109xxxx

The more keen-eyed of you will have noticed that not five pages ago I was advocating that you bid 3NT with one suit wide open and here I am suggesting you paint pretty pictures. Why? In the previous example we had no real chance of game at all. 5♣ was clearly not going to make unless partner found a couple of extra tricks more than you would expect for his opening. 3NT was unlikely to be a great contract either as it was eminently possible that the opposition had enough diamond tricks to cash. Thus the only sensible options were to pass or to bid an immediate, swashbuckling 3NT and make them have to find the necessary lead.

That is not the case at all here. With this hand we are sure to have a fair play for game provided partner has anything at all sensible for a 3♣ bid. It is not necessary to charge into 3NT with a suit wide open because 5♣ or even 6♣ could be cold depending on partner's hand. You would look particular silly if you bid 3NT and watched the opposition cash five heart tricks when you have 12 ice-cold tricks in clubs. Hence, on this hand you have the strength to explore. Thus you can safely bid 3◊.

(f)

♠ AKxx
♡ AQx
◊ xx
♣ AJxx

Answer: 3♡

This is considerably more dangerous than bidding 3◊ on the previous hand but nevertheless it has to be done. It is more dangerous because partner will strain to try and support a major much more than they will strain to support a minor, so you will get raised more often. But that is not so terrible. If you get raised to 4♡ then you can retreat again to 5♣ and that should have some play. It is true now that 3NT could have been better but you cannot have everything after a pre-empt. Notice that it would be quite wrong on this hand to bid 3♠. You do not want to play in spades. If partner raises them you will be go back to 5♣ anyway. The only point of bidding a major on this hand is to get partner to bid 3NT with a diamond stop. 3♡ will achieve this, 3♠ probably will not. Partner will bend over backwards to raise spades since they will feel this must be a genuine suit. After all, you cannot be probing for no trumps with two open suits, as you can hardly have stops in two suits for a pre-empt. Hence you should bid 3♡ so that partner can pinpoint your weakness in diamonds.

(g)
♠ AQJx
♡ xxx
◊ xx
♣ Qxxx

Answer: ?

Here we have no game ambition at all and are considerably worried about the opponents being able to make game themselves. Shouldn't we just pre-empt in clubs then and let the opponents get on with it? There is certainly nothing at all wrong with this approach and a straightforward 5♣ or 4♣ could well be the winner in the long run.

However, an enormously popular idea amongst the cognoscenti at the moment is to bid 3♠ on these sort of hands. This is not so much a psyche as an attempt to direct the defence.

The idea is that if you just raise clubs then partner will be in the dark about the opening lead and will almost certainly fish out a club, unless they have something a lot more attractive such as a singleton. It is difficult to believe that a club lead is going to do a lot for the defence. What is desperately needed is a spade lead. Hopefully this will be through the king but even if not it is liable to set up two tricks for the defence, something that a club lead is never going to do. The only way to get a spade lead is to bid them, so you do. This is actually quite safe since, if partner is unkind enough to raise, you simply return back to clubs where you intended to be all the time. All that you have done is got the defence off to a good start, which must be a good idea. Hence the popularity of such bids at the moment.

There are many situations where this kind of lead-directing bid can be used, particularly after pre-empts, and I will be exploring a few of them briefly later on. However, do not go around thinking these kind of bids have no downside. There is no such thing as a free lunch and certainly not a free lead-directing bid. As is always the case when you do something other than raise partner you increase the options for the opposition and hence they have more chance of doing the right thing. Bid 5♣ on this hand and the opposition have one bite of the cherry. They have to get it right then and there. Bid 3♠ and the opposition can double that, bid 4♣, bid a suit, bid 3NT or pass and bid later. Far more options and therefore more chances for the opposition to get it right.

It is all very well painting pictures about how the defence should go, but it isn't a lot of use if instead the opposition unkindly decide to double you or play a level lower than otherwise due to the room created by your bid. Bids such as 3♠ on the hand above can show spectacular successes and are very visible when they direct the only winning defence. I shall be interested to see if over the long run that outweighs the disadvantage of giving the opposition extra room. You will need to make up your own mind about that but it is certainly worth trying a few to see how they work for you.

Before we leave this hand I had better mention that there is a school of thought than suggests that all bids such as:

$$3\clubsuit \qquad \text{Pass} \qquad 3\spadesuit$$

and, even more so, bids such as:

$$3\spadesuit \qquad \text{Pass} \qquad 4\diamondsuit$$

should *guarantee* a fit for the pre-emptor's suit. Thus after 3♣–Pass it is fine to bid 3♠ on:

> ♠ AQJx
> ♡ xxx
> ◇ xx
> ♣ Qxxx

and partner will know that you have a club fit. But it cannot be bid on for example:

> ♠ AJ10xxxx
> ♡ xx
> ◇ Axx
> ♣ x

since we have no club fit. Similarly, after 3♠–Pass it would be perfectly acceptable to bid 4◇ on:

> ♠ Kxx
> ♡ xx
> ◇ AQJxx
> ♣ xxx

but not on:

> ♠ x
> ♡ x
> ♡ AKQJxxxx
> ♣ AQx

The technical term for this method is fit non-jump (FNJ for short). I rarely have a go at any methods but I personally find this particular idea completely bonkers. It seems to me that all of the rest of your bidding is messed up by this single insistence that all bids guarantee support for partner, a hand type which is not the most difficult to deal with anyway. If, however, you are interested in these ideas there are a huge number of areas in which they can be employed. A very full description of fit non-jumps, fit jumps and a million other ways of showing support for partner can be found in Oliver Segal and Andy Robson's book *Partnership Bidding*. I warn you though it is not easy going. It is the bridge equivalent of a maths text book.

(h)   ♠ Axxx
                           ♡ xx
                           ◇ xxx
                           ♣ Kxxx

Answer: 5♣

Why not? It is certainly the straight person's bid and the kind of effort I have been recommending. 4♣? OK, that may just work as well. Occasionally you can try 3♡. Most of the time they will pick up this baby psyche easily. But just occasionally you will find them with the right hands where it is not obvious to either opponent that you are not genuine; a flat 12 count with four hearts on your right and a 14 count with five hearts on your left, for example. You may be able to pick off their suit and play 3NT, 4♡ or 5♣ undoubled. It is also remarkably surprising how many pairs have no method for exposing such psyches or have never discussed what the bids mean. For example, are you sure that you and your partner know what:

3♣	Pass	3♡	Dble

means? Is it a take out double for spades and diamonds or is it penalties, showing hearts and exposing a psyche? Or does it just show a good hand? What if you pass and bid 4♡ on the next round? What if you pass and double on the next round? If you do not have any agreement with your partner as to what these bids mean, the next time somebody produces a baby psyche like this against you you are heading for a very silly result.

Again, this is not the sort of bid that you should try on a regular basis. Indeed, if you do the EBU sends round its death squad to hang you from the nearest tree. Most of the time it doesn't work and most of the time it simply gives your opponents more room. You are much better off with 5♣, though occasionally you score a goal with 3♡. And anyway it pays to advertise. If everyone knows that you never ever ever psyche then you are a lot easier to play against that if everyone knows that you rarely psyche but just maybe ... once in a while you might. Incidentally the easiest player of all to play against is the one that psyches all the time. They score the odd success but overall produce a whole series of silly results.

Finally, before we move away from responding to 3♣ what do jumps in new suits mean? Well, jumps to game in any suit should clearly be played as a desire to see the dummy. That is, you put down your dummy regardless of what you have pre-empted on for both 3♣–Pass–4♠ and 3♣–Pass–5◇. That is not to say that the bids are necessarily strong or that the game bidder has any hope of making the contract. It may well be a further pre-empt. Thus after 3♣–Pass, bid 4♠ on:

> ♠ KQJxxxxx
> ♡ Ax
> ◇ x
> ♣ Ax

where you seem to have good play for 4♠ but a slam seems ridiculous, and also on:

> ♠ KQJxxxxx
> ♡ xx
> ◇ x
> ♣ xx

where you have no chance in 4♠ but the opposition would appear to be cold for game in hearts.

4NT after a three level pre-empt is sensibly played as Blackwood, of whatever variety takes your fancy. If you normally play Roman Key Card Blackwood then it is very sensible to continue playing that. However, there is an argument that you should play straight Blackwood after a pre-empt rather than RKCB. This argument runs that, if the Blackwood bidder has a fit for the pre-emptor, then often the king of the pre-empt suit is irrelevant as they already hold it or it can be found out by other means. If however, the Blackwood bidder has a very good suit of their own they wish to play in, then they will only be interested in aces and the king of the pre-empt suit maybe an irrelevance. There is also an argument that something more sophisticated than Blackwood should be played since most of the responses are wasted as a pre-emptor hardly ever has two aces and certainly no more than two. It is for your partnership to decide what the best approach is. Undoubtedly the simplest is to play whatever you normally play. Anything else requires some systemic discussion and agreement.

This leaves us with jumps not to game. With a three level pre-empt the only possible sequence is:

3♣	Pass	4♢

However, when we come to look at weak twos there will be a number of possible sequences such as:

2♠	Pass	4♣/4♢

or:

2♡	Pass	3♠	etc.

How should these be played? There are really three sensible options. Firstly one can play them as showing a very good suit with slam interest. Partner can co-operate with a cuebid on any faintly suitable hand. Secondly they can be played as a splinter. Good support for the pre-emptor and shortage in the suit bid. Thirdly they can be played as showing a decent suit (though possibly not very long) together with a fit for the pre-emptor. Initially they are treated as purely lead-directional, though they may turn out to be stronger later on. This third option is an example of the fit-jump. We saw the fit non-jump mentioned previously.

Of these options, the first is my least favourite, both because it is rare (you need a really good hand opposite a pre-empt) and because it is unnecessary as you can simply bid your suit (forcing) and then you can invent a forcing bid if you need one on the next round of the auction. Both of the other options have merit in my opinion. Playing such bids as splinters is perfectly sensible and may enable you to bid some good slams as a result. It is also easy on the memory if you regularly play jumps in a lot of other situations as splinters.

The fit jump idea also has merit and again can be very effective in directing a defence. There are also negative inferences available when partner does not make a fit jump but simply raises your suit to an equivalent level. Now you know partner does not have a good lead, so it is often appropriate to lead the partnership suit and remain passive unless you have a very attractive lead yourself. However, the downside of the fit jump is again that it gives information, and more importantly room, to the opposition. I have much more sympathy for it in this case though as the bid is not necessary for other purposes. The problem I have with fit non-jumps is that I cannot see how sensibly to bid any hand without a fit if everything promises a fit.

So far I have concentrated entirely on responding to three of a minor pre-empt and ignored three of a major. This has been quite deliberate for the simple reason that it is, on the whole, easier to bid over three of a major than three of a minor. There are essentially three reasons for this:

(a) With a good hand you now have the very easy option of playing game in partner's major. This is usually the correct thing to do. It is well known that good hands facing poor hands with a long suit should generally play in that long suit so that it can actually take some tricks! Thus, you do not have to try probing for 3NT or game in your own major to such an extent. Most of the time raising partner's major will get the job done.

(b) With a bad hand you now have the very easy option of playing game in partner's major. Didn't I just say something like that? A wonderful advantage of a major suit pre-empt is that a single raise is game and you will make that single raise on a completely pre-emptive hand containing Qxx of trumps and a collection of tram tickets; a hand where you think you may have a play for game on a good day but not much defence; a distributional hand that will have to take a push to the five level if they bid; a really good hand that will 'lever the opposition all round the room and back again' (to borrow a phrase from John Helme) if they bid and a whole variety of others. Provided you can manage to raise on all these hand types in pretty much the same tempo you will leave the opposition completely in the dark about your hand. Sometimes they will not come in when they should do. Sometimes they will come in when you have a flat 18 count; 1100 points later they discover that was the wrong thing to do. Raising a major suit pre-empt to game forces the opposition to play at the five level in a minor over hearts and at the five level in anything over spades.

(c) A major suit pre-empt by its nature is much more destructive than a minor suit one. 3♠ removes the entire three level from the opposition and, if you raise, the four level is gone as well. 3♡ and, if possible, a raise to 4♡ means the opposition have to play five level if they do not happen to have spades. This can be a pain on occasion when you have a highly complex hand that requires a lot of exploration. On these occasions leaning across to partner and saying 'By the way, don't pre-empt on this hand will you' is about the only thing that will work – and that only until the Laws and Ethics Committee get hold of you. However, most of the time a raise to four of partner's major is fine and you can usually get away with that.

Before we move on to look at some hands, it is worth while pointing out that whatever your pre-emptive style you should allow considerably more latitude to major suit pre-empts than minor suit pre-empts and particularly to 3♠.

In particular, almost all partnerships now consider non-vulnerable three level major suit pre-empts on decent six card suits as simply routine. A number of partnerships have entirely different criteria for opening minor suit pre-empts to major suit pre-empts. Various possibilities exist. I have seen partnerships who play as extreme a variation as minor pre-empts promise KQ to seven as a minimum and major suit pre-empts can be jack to six and nothing else.

The reasons are essentially those outlined above. It is much easier to bid a sensible game after a major suit pre-empt than a minor suit pre-empt, hence you do not have to be so careful with them as you are less likely to get in partner's way to a significant extent.

You are not looking so yearnfully at 3NT after a major suit pre-empt so you do not need to worry so much about suit quality or length. With a good hand opposite, four of the major is likely to make anyway whereas the running suit may be essential in 3NT.

Most importantly of all, major suit pre-empts (and particularly 3♠) are simply so much more effective than minor suit ones as they remove the three level from the opposition. Hence you want to try and open them as much as possible, even in a sound pre-emptive style.

As usual, this is something you need to agree firmly with your partner. It matters that you are both on the same wavelength here. It is no good you solidly opening 3♠ on AQJxxxx if partner is going to pass, thinking you will have Jxxxxxx. Similarly it is no good your opening 3♠ on Jxxxxxx if partner is going to raise on a singleton confidently expecting a one loser suit.

Let's look at some hands, assuming that partner has opened 3♠ at Green in a sound style. I'll use the same hands as before with the black suits rearranged.

Firstly the hands on which we bid 3NT last time. Re-arranging the black suits gives:

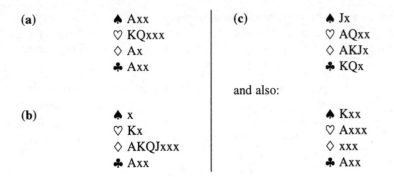

(a)
- ♠ Axx
- ♡ KQxxx
- ◇ Ax
- ♣ Axx

Answer: 4♠

True 3NT could be the only making contract but if the spades do not run you will look very silly. 4♠ must have good play, so why take the risk?

(b)
- ♠ x
- ♡ Kx
- ◇ AKQJxxx
- ♣ Axx

Answer: 3NT

This hand is still a 3NT bid. On a heart lead you still have nine tricks. This seems to me to be a lot more likely that avoiding four losers in 4♠.

(c)
- ♠ Jx
- ♡ AQxx
- ◇ AKJx
- ♣ KQx

Answer 4♠

4♠ is going to be much superior to 3NT here just as 5♣ was superior to 3NT.

What about another hand we have seen before?

♠ Kxx
♡ Axxx
◇ xxx
♣ Axx

I still have a sneaking admiration for 3NT on this hand. You really do not expect to make any game on this hand and if you do get a game on the card, then 3NT is much the most likely. The trouble is that it could be a very silly result indeed. Partners, as we have discussed, are much more likely to pre-empt on less than wonderful suits in majors than in minors. You will look very silly in 3NT facing queen to seven spades. Worse, it is possible that 4♠ will be cold (whereas it was inconceivable that 5♣ was cold). Give partner a highly suitable hand such as:

♠ QJxxxxx
♡ KJx
◇ x
♣ xx

and game seems to be on the heart finesse. Thus again the 4♠ bid wins the day. Notice that again I do not even consider Pass as an alternative. It is true that 3♠ may be the limit of your hands. It could even be too high. Do you really want to put this down to find out? Worse, do you really want to defend 4♡ or even 3NT (someone could have ♠Axx)? Stop trying to land on a pin head. Let the opposition have the problem.

Moving on to the hands on which we raised partner's pre-empt as our preferred option last time.

Rearranging the black suits gives:

(a)
♠ Kxx
♡ x
◇ Axxxx
♣ xxxx

(b)
♠ Kxxx
♡ x
◇ Q98xxx
♣ xx

(c)
♠ Kxx
♡ xx
◇ Axxxx
♣ xxx

(d)
♠ Qxx
♡ xxxx
◇ xxx
♣ xxx

(e)   ♠ QJ   (f)   ♠ J10
            ♡ xxx   ♡ AQx
            ◊ 1087xxx   ◊ Q10xx
            ♣ Ax   ♣ KJxx

Of these:

(a) Is a clear 4♠ bid as I hope by now will be obvious. You don't expect to make 4♠, but you do expect the opposition to make 4♡.

(b) Can also bid 4♠. However, this is going to keep nobody out! You have such a weak hand with such good support for partner that nobody is going to allow you to play at anything like this low a level. 5♠ is much more of a bid to give them a headache. Now they have to start bidding at the six level and may well just choose to double instead which is fine by you. 6♠ is also a possibility. Here you force the opposition into doubling you (nobody starts the auction at the seven level!). 6♠ is a bid that says you are certain the opposition are cold for a slam and that they will have bid it. Quite a compliment to them! That is why my personal preference is for 5♠. You may be doubled a level lower.

(c) Is also a clear 4♠ bid. You expect the opposition to be able to make game and you expect your side to make about seven or eight tricks. A good save, so bid it quickly.

(d) I would also bid 4♠ on this hand. True, you now expect a penalty of about -800 but it is worth it to take away the four level from the opposition. The opposition would appear to be odds on for a slam and the extra level of pre-emption may be all that is needed to prevent them getting there. They may well stop at the five level or they may choose to take the penalty. Notice how much more effective raising 3♠ to 4♠ is than raising 3♣ to 4♣. With spades the entire four level is gone for the opposition, with clubs it is all still there.

(e) Is again a 4♠ bid for the usual reasons. You expect 4♠ to be a good save, so bid it.

(f) Is a clear pass. Unless your pre-empts are hyper-sound you do not expect to have any chance in 4♠ so just pass 3♠. Unlike last time you will tempt nobody in with a clever raise either. Nobody is tempted in at the five level; they only bid at that level if they really want to.

Finally, what about hands where we introduced a suit last time?

Re-arranging the black suits again gives:

(a)	♠ Ax ♡ KQJxxx ◊ xx ♣ AKx	(e)	♠ AJx ♡ xx ◊ AQxx ♣ AKxx
(b)	♠ A ♡ AKQJxxxx ◊ xx ♣ AK	(f)	♠ AJxx ♡ AQx ◊ xx ♣ AKxx
(c)	♠ – ♡ AKQxx ◊ xx ♣ KQJxxx	(g)	♠ Qxxx ♡ xxx ◊ xx ♣ AQJx
(d)	♠ xx ♡ x ◊ Axx ♣ AJ10xxxx	(h)	♠ Axxx ♡ xx ◊ xxx ♣ Kxxx

(a)

♠ Ax
♡ KQJxxx
◊ xx
♣ AKx

Answer: 4♠

Yes, it is true that you can construct hands where 4♡ is better than 4♠ but there are far more hands where 4♠ is much, much better than 4♡. And you have to make the decision now. You cannot bid 4♡ as a 'choice of contracts' as I have heard players claim in the post-mortem when they have gone three down in a 6-0 fit. 4♡ is a request to see the dummy. If you had a void in spades and eight solid hearts you would bid 4♡ and would not be enamoured of the buffoon who bid 4♠. Hence you should raise to 4♠. You are sure of a 7-2 or 6-2 fit, you have ample values for game and it is usually right to play in the weak hand's long suit. You are not guaranteed to make this but it must be worth a shot. Notice the difference between the opening of 3♣ and 3♠. Over 3♣ we bid 3♡ as 4♡ was the most likely game. Over 3♠ we can forget about hearts, we already have found a major suit fit.

'The secret of success at bridge is to own the spade suit and use it judiciously'. So said the Great Philosopher Kokish.

(b)
          ♠ A
          ♡ AKQJxxxx
          ◇ xx
          ♣ AK

Answer: ?

Thank you, partner! Here we have been completely stuffed by partner's bid. How on earth are we going to find out what we need from partner? One possibility is just to bid 4NT and bid 6♡ if partner has an ace or settle for 5♡ otherwise. But if you follow that route you had better have agreed that 4NT was straight Blackwood rather than RKCB, otherwise you might be in the embarrassing position of bidding a slam with a cashing AK off it (and no way of disposing of them even if they do not lead them!). You could try 5♡ as a general slam try. This will certainly get partner to bid 6♡ with the ◇A. If s/he is feeling on form s/he might manage it with a singleton diamond and a few low hearts, as well. Though how partner is supposed to know that a diamond singleton makes the hand laydown and a club singleton is about as useful as a chocolate teapot I do not know. The other option is simply to shrug your shoulders, decide that you have been fixed by the idiot opposite and just bid 4♡. I have considerable sympathy with this view and it is the approach I would certainly take if I could not guarantee 11 tricks in my hand. Change the hand for example to:

          ♠ K
          ♡ AKQJxxxx
          ◇ xx
          ♣ AK

and you couldn't get me to bid more than 4♡. True you could still make 6♡ (♠A and a singleton diamond from partner) but advance beyond 4♡ and you can bet partner will table ♠QJ109xxx and three low diamonds. The aim after pre-empts is to get a plus score and that is as true after your own pre-empts as it is after the opposition's. Here, however, your hand is so powerful that 4♡ does seem just a little lily-livered. I still think it is a sensible option though, given that you have no bid that will enable you to get the necessary information out of partner, to bid the slam with confidence. Notice also that here is an example of a hand where you want to play in 4♡. You do not want your partner to bid 4♠ because 'I thought it would be better'. You want them to put their dummy down before they do any more damage. 4♡ does not offer a choice of contracts.

(c)
♠ –
♡ AKQxx
◇ xx
♣ KQJxxx

Answer: Pass

Thanks again, partner! They are really choosing their moment well here. Again it is possible to construct hands where 4♡ will make but they really are few and far between. Despite appearances you are likely to make considerably more tricks in spades than in hearts. Unless partner has some magic holding such as ♡Jxx you are likely to get forced early on and your club suit may well go in the bin. It is not impossible that you will make five heart tricks and nothing else on this hand. Whereas in spades partner will limit the losers to however many diamonds they hold, the ♣A and whatever spade losers there are. Probably a couple off is the expectation. Rather better and a level lower. If you pass smoothly on this hand sometimes the opposition come to your rescue. They might bid 3NT (and then you will have to decide if you have the bottle to double it to see if you can get partner to lead the right suit). They might bid diamonds. Worst of all they might double and pass it back to you. Now you have to decide if you want to jump from the frying pan of 3♠ doubled to the possible fire of 4♣ (oh yes, they will certainly double you). Nevertheless pass is clearly the percentage option initially.

(d)
♠ xx
♡ x
◇ Axx
♣ AJ10xxxx

Answer: 4♠

You do not really expect to make this but you might. It is certainly possible to construct hands for partner that will make 4♠ in comfort. However, I would have thought the expectation would be nine tricks. Why then do we bid a contract we do not expect to make? Well why do you think? You've got a nine count with a singleton heart and partner has pre-empted. Do you really think they are going to pass you out quietly in 3♠? In your dreams. And what are you going to do when they bid 4♡? Do you fancy your chances against that? Sure you might beat it on say ♣A and a ruff, ◇A and a trick in the wash but do you really fancy defending it? Surely you are going to bid 4♠ as a sensible save. In which case you should bid it now, before the opposition know what is going on, before the opposition have a chance to define their hands and before you have told them that you do not think you can make 4♠. Quite often you will get clean away with 4♠. It will just be passed out and probably drift off. You could have a good hand like (e) or (f) below rather than this old rope. Occasionally you will get doubled. But you have shut out 4♡. The opposition now will have to bid 5♡ if they want to play in those. This you will let play. You might even double it. After all you do have two defensive tricks. It will not make any overtricks. A singleton club or any trick in partner's hand will beat it. And perhaps most important of all you give notice to the opposition that, if they come in over your pre-empts on the wrong hand, then they are going to pay for it. All this for the price of 5 IMPs if you double it and it makes. Those are pretty good odds.

4♠ is a good example of what experts refer to all the time as a two-way shot. You might make 4♠ (though you probably will not). They might make 4♡ (they probably will). Either of these outcomes make it right to bid 4♠ and you do not care which it is. The only way passing 3♠ is right is if both 4♠ and 4♡ fail and that is really rather unlikely. So go ahead and bid 4♠. Apart from anything else it is just easier on the heart and mind. You do not have to agonise over whether to save over 4♡ or not. You bid 4♠ in tempo and let the opponent do the agonising. Bid 4♠ and live a healthier life!

Another option which many would recommend on this hand is 4♣. The idea here is again that partner will get off to the best lead if the opposition buy the hand. Also partner will be able to judge the degree of fit better and may be able to save over 4♡, pass to suggest no direction or even double. Hence we draw partner into the decision. On the whole these consultative bids are very sensible. In this case I think it is an 'expert stupidity'. The problem with 4♣ is that you know LHO is going to bid 4♡. Well, perhaps 'know' is going a bit far but they will do so with a high degree of frequency and you have just given LHO a golden chance to get the suit in at the level they most wanted to, the four level. Well, let's have a round of applause for the juggler! You could have given them a real headache as to whether to bid at the five level or not but instead you give them a free shot at the four level and then they can decide whether to pass you out in 4♠, double you or bid 5♡. Bravo! If the majors had been reversed, however (i.e. partner had opened 3♡ and we were 1-2 in the majors), then I can see a lot of merit in 4♣ and I think it is the right bid. The difference here is that 4♡ will not keep out the spade suit. If anything it will goad the opponents into 4♠. So in this case you can bid 4♣ and you can take advantage of the extra information you have available to decide whether to save over 4♠ (notice that 5♣ may well be much superior to 5♡), pass them out (most probable) or even, on a really good day, double. If you have hearts they have the boss suit and it is you who have to decide whether to bid at the five level or not.

(e)
　　　　　　　　　　　　♠ AJx
　　　　　　　　　　　　♡ xx
　　　　　　　　　　　　◇ AQxx
　　　　　　　　　　　　♣ AKxx

Answer: 4♠

An easy one. Bid 4♠, collect ten or eleven tricks and pass onto the next hand. If the opposition feel like bidding tell them that it isn't a good idea, ring up your bank manager and double.

(f)
　　　　　　　　　　　　♠ AJxx
　　　　　　　　　　　　♡ AQx
　　　　　　　　　　　　◇ xx
　　　　　　　　　　　　♣ AKxx

Answer: 4♠

Another easy one. Again bid 4♠, collect ten or eleven tricks and pass onto the next hand.

(g)
　　　　　　　　　　　　♠ Qxxx
　　　　　　　　　　　　♡ xxx
　　　　　　　　　　　　◇ xx
　　　　　　　　　　　　♣ AQJx

Answer: 4♠

Don't even think of anything else! Certainly not 4♣ which gives the opposition all the room in the world. Bid 4♠ and let them get on with it. Again you can try a clever 4♣ if you want when your suit is hearts but not when it is spades. Take away the four level as fast as you can.

(h)   ♠ Axxx
                                     ♡ xx
                                     ◇ xxx
                                     ♣ Kxxx

Answer: 4♠

Another obvious 4♠ bid.

Have you noticed how many hands we have bid 4♠ over 3♠ on? All told it is 13 hands out of 18, ranging from flat 3 counts to flat 17 counts. That's why a raise to game can be so effective. It says nothing about your hand-type.

So far, we have concentrated solely on non-vulnerable pre-empts. This I have done deliberately. Vulnerability is one of the aspects we noted earlier as having a significant effect on pre-empts. At Green your pre-empts, whatever their style, are at their loosest with the lowest constraints on them. Conversely, at Red your pre-empts, whatever their style, are at their most constrained. The most important constraint in almost everybody's opinion is suit quality. Vulnerable pre-empts, and particularly vulnerable against not pre-empts, require a good suit. It is simply far too dangerous to go around pre-empting on poor or moderate suits vulnerable. If you get doubled you will go for a fortune and, even if you just get passed out, undertricks in 100s add up remarkably fast. You are getting a below par result even undoubled unless the opposition have a game on.

Quite what constitutes a good suit is for partnerships to decide for themselves. However, a common rule that partnerships often use is that a vulnerable pre-empt requires a seven card suit to two of the top three honours and reasonable intermediates. That is, KQ98xxx is a minimum vulnerable pre-empt.

The extra constraints on vulnerable pre-empts have an effect on the responder's bidding. The responder can be sure of a good suit and good playing strength. Hence responder should strain even more than before to support opener's suit with a good hand since the hand will almost always play best in opener's suit. In addition slam tries can be made more freely secure in the knowledge that vulnerable pre-empts will deliver some tricks and playing strength. To illustrate quite what can happen, let's take a look at an old hand from the great days of the all conquering Italian Blue Team. Your partner Giorgio Belladonna (you should be so lucky) opens 3♠ at Red and you hold:

♠ Q73
♡ 865
◇ A5
♣ AKQ96

What do you do? Most players I know would simply raise this to 4♠ happy that this will be such a good contract. But if you think about this it is incredibly lazy. If partner had opened 3♠ at Green then certainly simply raising to 4♠ is not unreasonable. You need an awful lot from partner to make a slam. Firstly you need a heart control, secondly you need the trump suit to play for no losers opposite your Qxx. True, this is entirely possible but it is also possible that partner has KJxxxx(x). Even if partner has AK to six you still may not have enough tricks; six spades, ace of diamonds and four clubs (why should the clubs come in for five tricks?) still only makes 11 tricks. Worse, making some fancy bid may tip the opponents off to the correct lead. Give partner a perfectly good non-vulnerable pre-empt such as:

♠ KJxxxx
♡ xxx
◇ x
♣ xx

and you can see what will happen if you bid 4♣. Partner will co-operate with 4◇, you will bid 4♠, the opposition will lead a heart without even looking at their hand and that will be the end of that. True the opposition may lead a heart anyway if you just bid 4♠ but at least you have given yourself a chance. It is still not a wonderful game on a non-heart lead but a 3-3 club break or someone having to ruff with the singleton ace of trumps will see you home. So on balance a 4♠ call is probably the sensible action.

However, all this changes when partner has opened 3♠ vulnerable, and particularly at Red. Above we said that partner needs a heart control, a no loser suit opposite Qxx and seven spades to ensure 12 tricks. All this was too much to ask. But it is not too much to ask from a vulnerable pre-empt! The last two of these are more or less guaranteed. For a vulnerable pre-empt partner will almost always have seven to two of the top three honours. Hence you can virtually place partner with ♠AKxxxxx. Now you can begin to see why bidding 4♠ opposite a vulnerable pre-empt is such a very lazy bid. If partner has a heart control then you can underwrite a slam. The Italians were not world champions for twenty years by making lazy bids like 4♠. What however impresses me about this hand is not that the Italians were able to reach a slam but that they bid confidently to the *grand* slam. Yes a grand slam was cold since partner held:

♠ AK98432
♡ –
♦ 7632
♣ J5

A perfectly sensible vulnerable pre-empt and 13 ice-cold tricks. Thus do not underestimate the power of knowing that a good seven card suit is opposite you.

Responding to Second in Hand Pre-empts

There is no real difference to responding to second in hand pre-empts than first in hand ones except that you need to bear in mind than partner should be sounder for a second in hand pre-empt than a first in hand one. This will not matter much if you have a sound pre-emptive style except that partner will be even less likely to try something a little weaker than expected second in hand. For all the reasons discussed in Chapter 1 it is nonsense to produce very wild pre-empts second in hand. One opponent has passed so they can sort out their assets better and you are just as likely to give partner a headache as you are LHO. Thus, even if you believe in pre-empts on jack to five producing these second in hand is just silly. Hence most partnerships have stronger criteria for second in hand pre-empts than first in hand pre-empts and you should take this into account when responding to second in hand pre-empts. The exact limits for second in hand pre-empts are a partnership matter but many pairs play that, even with a very wild style first in hand, a minimum of KJxxxx is required for a second in hand pre-empt for example. If you decide on a rule such as this then you need to bear this in mind when responding to second in hand pre-empts. You need have no fears any more of partner producing six small or queen to five. You can bid 3NT on ace to three in partner's suit with the expectation that you will be able to run the suit most of the time. And so on.

Responding to Third in Hand Pre-empts

This one is easy. On the whole, don't! Whatever your pre-emptive style it makes sense to give partner a lot of leeway for a third in hand pre-empt. If partner has a bad hand then fourth in hand must have a good one, so partner should be allowed to have a go at disrupting this good hand without you getting in the way. Hence almost all partnerships allow most things for a third in hand pre-empt. Partner may have less cards that your advertised style; partner may have a poorer suit than normal; partner may have an outside four card major even if you do not normally do so in your style; partner may actually be stronger than normal and just trying to take up some room (see the example in Chapter 1); partner may be two suited and even exceptionally a canapé. I once saw a spectacularly successful 3♠ opener third in hand on:

♠ AQ10xx
♡ –
♢ J109xxxx
♣ x

vulnerable to boot! Hardly classical but it worked on the combination of cards around the table. So your main job in responding to third in hand pre-empts is not to get in partner's way. Partner may well have taken an off-centre decision to try and cause the opponents some grief and will not thank you if you take some overly aggressive action opposite. Overall, this means again that you should not raise partner so freely. Ideally you want four card support to raise partner's pre-empt since partner will quite likely only have six whatever your style. If you have only three card support then there had better be some compensating reason such as a distributional value or a decent side suit.

Remember also that you will be known to be weak. You cannot get away any more with raising 3♠ to 4♠ and the opposition not knowing whether you have a flat 18 count or a flat 6 count. This time they will be able to work it out. Thus you only want to raise partner when you are fairly sure that it will be a good save. You are very likely to be doubled and have to play there, so you want to be certain that this is the right thing to do. It is also almost never right to raise partner if your RHO passes. Now both opponents have passed and it is likely that the hand will be passed out. Most of the time you can pass and hope and it will be alright. Raising in these situations simply is a chance to incur a bigger minus score.

So for example, with:

♠ Qxx
♡ xxx
♢ xxx
♣ AQJx

I would not raise to 4♠ after the auction:

Pass	Pass	3♠	Pass
?			

Neither of the opposition seems to want to bid and the hand may be passed out. It is unlikely you can make 4♠ and you may have enough for partner to make 3♠. Partner will not be happy going one off in 4♠ when the opponents can make nothing. I am not advocating that you never raise partner's third in hand pre-empt if there is pass on your right, merely that you are circumspect about it. For example on:

♠ Axxx
♡ x
◇ KJxxx
♣ xxxx

I would always raise 3♠ to 4♠ regardless of who does what and I am sure you would as well. It is surprising that nobody has found the heart suit yet but give them enough time and they surely will. It is possible of course that partner has a few of them but that will just increase the value of your singleton heart. Besides, never mind what the opponents can make, there are plenty of hands opposite that will make 4♠ so go ahead and bid it.

It should be clear that you will not be doing anything other than raising partner. It is difficult to see how a passed hand can be gaily introducing a new suit at the three level. For this reason, whatever your methods over a first or second hand pre-empt any new suit you bid over a third in hand pre-empt promises support for the pre-empt. In this context it is sensible to use these bids as lead-directional a lot of the time and again these bids are much in vogue at the moment. I would advise caution as usual in that they do allow the opposition extra room so use them wisely. So for example, on:

♠ AQJx
♡ xxx
◇ xx
♣ Qxxx

it is sensible to try 3♠ after the sequence:

Pass	Pass	3♣	Dble
?			

You definitely want a spade lead if LHO plays the contract. You do not really want to bash 5♣ at this stage as the opposition will certainly double that and you expect -300 or -500 with no game guaranteed for the opposition yet. 3♠ from a passed hand which must promise a club fit will allow partner a chance to judge the auction. They may choose to save with a fit. For example:

♠ Kxx
♡ x
♢ xxx
♣ KJxxxx

or:

♠ xxx
♡ xx
♢ x
♣ AJxxxxx

are both excellent saves against 4♡. They may choose to pass with no real direction. For example:

♠ xx
♡ xx
♢ xxx
♣ KJ10xxx

would pass and lead a spade since the save does not look attractive and there seems no prospect of beating 4♡. On a good day partner might even double if the opponents bid 4♡. For example:

♠ x
♡ Ax
♢ xxx
♣ Axxxxxx

is a clear-cut double after the auction:

Pass	Pass	3♣	Dble
3♠	4♡	?	

The opposition have eight hearts, a combined 23 count and some distribution between them. Usually enough to have a go at game and yet you can whack them with considerable confidence thanks to partner's 3♠ call. See how useful these lead-directional bids can be? This last example is hardly a classic pre-empt with two aces and a bad suit, I hear you say. I agree and no-one would make such a bid first or second in hand. However, many players would give it a shot third in hand. Occasionally you get results like these.

On the other hand I would not bid 4♣ on:

♠ Qxxx
♡ xxx
♢ xx
♣ AQJx

after the auction:

Pass	Pass	3♠	Dble
?			

Here you are reasonably confident that 4♠ is a good save and you would certainly want to take it if the opposition bid 4♡. On the other hand you will not want to try 5♠ if the opponents bid to the five level. Hence I think you should just bid 4♠ and force an immediate decision on your LHO. 4♣ gives them too many options as to whether to bid 4♡ and then 5♡, bid 4♡ and double 4♠ or just double 4♠. It also allows diamonds into the auction far too easily.

Responding to Fourth in Hand Pre-empts

This of course depends on what style of fourth in hand pre-empts you intend to adopt. If, as I have suggested that you play fourth in hand pre-empts as showing very good suits then your bidding problems are relatively straightforward. You bid 3NT or another game if you think you can make it and pass otherwise. Look back at Chapter 1 for a couple of examples of bidding over fourth in hand pre-empts. Do not worry about the opponents after a fourth in hand pre-empt either. Remember both of them have passed. Unless you are playing against John Collings most opponents who are happy to pass the hand out do not start lurching into the auction at the three level. Hence pre-emptive raises are a thing of the past and new suits are logically game tries.

Thus it is entirely sensible to bid 3♠ on:

♠ Axx
♡ xxx
♢ Kxx
♣ Kxxx

after the auction:

Pass	Pass	Pass	3 ◊
Pass	?		

This will focus partner's mind on the need for a heart stop (else why not 3♡ from you) and you may be able to bid a cold game opposite, for example:

> ♠ x
> ♡ Ax
> ◊ AQJ10xxx
> ♣ xxx

On a really good day you may even be able to play 5 ◊ opposite say:

> ♠ Kx
> ♡ x
> ◊ AQJ10xxx
> ♣ J109

3

RESPONDING TO WILD AND RANDOM THREE LEVEL PRE-EMPTS

Responding to Wild Pre-empts

The reverse side of the coin to responding to sound vulnerable pre-empts is responding to wild non-vulnerable pre-empts. In the former case you can be sure partner has a good seven card suit. In the latter case you can be sure partner has 13 cards some of which are probably in the suit opened. It is a very different matter responding to a pre-empt if it might be KJxxxx and out, or worse Qxxxxx and out, or worse still Jxxxx and out. This must alter your entire philosophy to responding in a number of ways.

Firstly and obviously you should be much less aggressive with good hands. If you have a good hand and partner opens an aggressive pre-empt then you just have to shrug your shoulders and accept that partner has picked a bad moment to do this. You do not go around trying to bid games on the hope that partner has a suitable hand for you. Partner won't. Partner never has a suitable hand when you take an aggressive action; partner only ever has a suitable hand when you take an unaggressive action. You know that as well as I do; it's just life.

Nowhere is this difference so visible than in the hands on which you bid 3NT over a minor suit pre-empt. You should still bid 3NT over a wild pre-empt every time you think you can make it, but you now think you can make it so much less often!

Let's look at the hands we considered last time for bidding 3NT and assume this time that partner has opened a wild 3♣ at Green.

(a)
$\spadesuit$ Axx
$\heartsuit$ KQxxx
$\diamondsuit$ Ax
$\clubsuit$ Axx

Is now a clear cut pass. 3NT is very much odds against opposite a wild pre-empt. True partner may just put down $\clubsuit$Kxxxxx and an outside king when a 2-2 club break will see you home. But I've given you a good wild pre-empt here and it is still only just about worth bidding non-vulnerable. Give partner $\clubsuit$Qxxxxx and out and 3NT is just looking ridiculous. Pass and hope 3$\clubsuit$ makes. Yes there is no guarantee that this is enough for 3$\clubsuit$. A hand such as:

$\spadesuit$ xxx
$\heartsuit$ x
$\diamondsuit$ xxx
$\clubsuit$ Qxxxxx

will do very well to put 3$\clubsuit$ on the card. Never underestimate just how much you need to move over a wild pre-empt or how much you need even to make the contract. That is one of the real downsides of a wild pre-emptive style; every time there is a good hand opposite you are usually already too high. The hope is that the opposition will have more good hands than your partner (there are two of them compared with one partner after all).

(b)
$\spadesuit$ Axx
$\heartsuit$ Kx
$\diamondsuit$ AKQJxxx
$\clubsuit$ x

is still a 3NT call obviously. On a heart lead you still have nine tricks, so get on with it. Apart from anything else you probably have more chance in 3NT than partner has in 3$\clubsuit$!

(c)
$\spadesuit$ KQx
$\heartsuit$ AQxx
$\diamondsuit$ AKJx
$\clubsuit$ Jx

presents us with the most problems. I know people who would pass hand (c) as well on the grounds that no game is likely to be very good. But passing this out in 3$\clubsuit$ is balancing the QE2 on a pinhead. I think you just have to bid 3NT here and hope that you have a play at it. Wild pre-empts are designed to force decisions on people. If you have the good hand then it is you that the decision is forced upon. Notice that here the option of trying 5♣ is just silly. You cannot expect to make 5♣ opposite what is likely to be a moth-eaten six card suit. Two trumps and the ♠A off the contract are likely before you start. Bid 3NT and hope partner has some useful minor honours outside clubs.

It is certainly the case that you can never get away with a 3NT call on a thin hand anymore. To bid 3NT on the example I suggested earlier:

> ♠ Axx
> ♡ Axxx
> ◇ xxx
> ♣ Kxx

is now plain bonkers (though it might work as a psyche I suppose). Even if you avoid the diamond lead the chance of partner providing a club suit to furnish you with seven tricks opposite king to three is more or less zero. Hand (a) above would be an example of a thin 3NT call opposite a wild pre-empt. At least with hand (a) you might make 3NT on a good day; with this hand it is merely a matter of how many you are going off.

Secondly, you need to be much more careful about pre-emptively raising partner. Qxx is fine support for a sound pre-empt and you can cheerfully raise the pre-empt happy in the knowledge that you have a highly robust trump suit at least. This is not the case after a wild pre-empt. If your style is to pre-empt on jack to six and out or king to five and out, then Qxx will still leave you with two or three trump losers. The most likely result of raising partner is that the opposition will take their easiest route to a large plus score by placing a red card on the table. This is the downside of wild pre-empts which is not often taken into consideration. You simply cannot afford to raise partner pre-emptively anywhere near as often.

The advocates of wild pre-empts will say that this is irrelevant. You pre-empt far more often than with sound pre-empts and you rely on the extra disruption which opening as often as possible at the three level will cause; the fact that you cannot raise the pre-empt as often is irrelevant since you are pre-empting so much more often. There is a lot of merit in this argument and I am not trying to gainsay it. I merely point out that the demerits as well as the merits of this style ought to be taken into account.

Thirdly, and less obviously, you need to be much more concerned about strain opposite a wild pre-empt than you are opposite a sound pre-empt. This is the case whether you have a good or a bad hand opposite the pre-empt. If you have a void in partner's suit then opposite a sound pre-empt that is just unfortunate and you hope you do not get doubled. It is unlikely though that you can make more tricks in another suit unless you have a very long suit of your own. However, if the pre-empt opposite can be queen to five, then owning a void by way of support is a disaster. In this case it is almost certain that you can make more tricks in another suit and possibly in all of them! The problem is that if you bid partner will regard this as forcing, as we know from previous discussions. Hence you cannot just try to improve the contract, since you are going to end up at least one level higher than previously. Unfortunate, to say the least!

There are various remedies to this. One is to shrug your shoulders, hope you do not get doubled, try and run as best you can when you do and accept that you are going for a fortune a lot of the time. An alternative is to change the style of responses to pre-empts. About the first pair in this country to do this were Graham Kirby and John Armstrong. This should come as no surprise since Kirby-Armstrong were also one of the first pairs in the country to play very wild pre-empts. Kirby-Armstrong's idea was simply to play all three level responses to pre-empts as non-forcing instead of forcing. So sequences such as:

	3♣	Pass	3♡

or:

	3♡	Pass	3♠

would be non-forcing. This is not to say that partner had to pass. With a suitable hand partner could raise. It is also not to say that they necessarily showed poor hands. True, hands will a good suit of their own and no fit for partner would bid just as an attempt to improve the contract. So, for example:

♠ xx
♡ KJ10xxxx
◊ Axxx
♣ −

would bid 3♡ over 3♣ just because it will be a better contract (you also want a heart lead if the opposition decide to play in 3NT). However these bids could also be genuinely constructive game tries. Thus you would equally bid 3♡ over 3♣ on:

♠ xxx
♡ AKJxxxx
◇ x
♣ Ax

where it is possible that 4♡ will make but you certainly do not wish to be higher than 3♡ if partner has a singleton heart and ♣Qxxxxx, for example.

I remember seeing one somewhat extreme example of this style when John Armstrong held:

♠ KJ10xxx
♡ Axx
◇ x
♣ AKx

and responded a non-forcing 3♠ to his partner's 3♣ opening! But if you stop and think about this for a moment it is entirely logical. You have a hand good enough that game is a possibility even opposite a wild pre-empt. *But not in clubs.* How is partner going to make 5♣ when the expectation for his pre-empt is queen to six and out on a good day? Depending on how many hearts partner has you may be on the spade finesse to make three clubs. Thus, if there is going to be a game it must be 4♠. Now it is certainly reasonable to pass that hand opposite a wild pre-empt and at least be fairly sure of a plus score. To try for the spade game with 3♠ is aggressive, but nobody has ever accused John Armstrong of being a wimp at the table, so he chose 3♠. Notice that this action would be impossible if 3♠ were forcing. You are guaranteed to get to at least 4♣ with no guarantee of it making. 3♠ was followed by three rapid passes and partner tabled the fine collection of:

♠ xx
♡ xxx
◇ Jx
♣ 109xxxx!

This drifted a couple off (the defence dropped a trick) but since the clubs were 3-1 3♣ had no play either, so it was hardly a big deal.

Now again there is a downside to this style. With no forcing bids available if you have a really good hand you virtually have to guess the final contract. You cannot develop the auction comfortably because there are no forcing bids available. In particular two suiters are a real problem as there is no guarantee that you will be able to bid both of your suits. You may be just left to play in the first one you bid when partner has much better support for the other one. But the argument is one of frequency. Hands that are sufficiently good to force to game opposite a wild pre-empt come up very rarely; you more or less need an Acol 2♣ opener. Hands which either simply want to improve the contract or make a non-forcing game try come up much more frequently. Hence it makes sense to play such bids as non-forcing.

Let's continue our discussion of how to respond to wild pre-empts by looking at a problem that appeared in one of the bridge magazines recently. It was as follows:

East/West Game. Pairs. Dealer North.

South
♠ J972
♡ A7
♢ AQ5
♣ AK95

South	West	North	East
–	–	3◇(i)	Pass
3NT	4♡	Pass	Pass
?			

    (i)   random style

The votes on this problem were 15 for 4NT and 7 for double. Yet I think they were wrong! If you look at the quotes from a number of the bridge stars who bid 4NT they include:

> *'It is hard to believe that partner, no matter how random, has less than ◇Kxxxxx.'*

> *'He certainly holds six to the king, even with the "Random style".'*

But it seems to me that these experts are refusing to take the problem as it was set. It may be that the test of time will show that random pre-empts are losing options and they will disappear. But until then to answer a problem by refusing to accept that such a bid exists makes no sense at all. Of course if we could guarantee partner had no 'less than Kxxxxx' we would all bid 4NT. We can all count up to ten top tricks. This simply would not be a problem. The problem is that seven diamonds cannot be guaranteed and nor can the king. It is a genuine problem if partner's diamond holding cannot be counted upon. If partner is as likely to hold ◊ xxxxxx as ◊ Kxxxxx then 3NT, let alone 4NT, has no play. In this case it was not with sanguinity that we bid 3NT. We had to bid it since ◊ Kxxxxx and out is nine tricks, but it wouldn't have surprised us if 3NT was going (a lot) down. Looked at in this way double seems more and more attractive. You have no guarantee of 4NT; you have excellent defence against 4♡; they are vulnerable; and the less diamond length partner can have the more likely your diamond trick is to stand up. Indeed on a really good day you will be able to cash two diamond tricks when partner has found an imaginative shot on king to five! Not surprising then my vote is strongly for double and it is interesting to observe the members of the panel who did vote for double. They included Hackett, Brock and Landy; aggressive pre-emptors all. Henry Bethe doubled with the comment:

> *'Don't know what 'Random Style' means ... does it mean it could be anything from 10xxxxx to KJxxxxx?'*

Exactly, Henry! The point again is that, if you are going to play a wild style of pre-empting, then you cannot go around assuming partner will have king, jack to seven for a pre-empt! You must assume partner has something more likely and more in the middle of the range such as king to six.

Moving on let's look again at the hands that we examined where we were dealing with sound pre-empts. This time we will assume that partner has opened a wild first in hand Green pre-empt and that we are playing non-forcing responses as detailed above. We have already examined the potential hands to bid 3NT on, so we will now look at the hands on which we raised partner:

(a)	♠ xxxx	(c)	♠ xxx
	♡ x		♡ xx
	◊ Axxxx		◊ Axxxx
	♣ Kxx		♣ Kxx
(b)	♠ xx	(d)	♠ xxx
	♡ x		♡ xxxx
	◊ Q987xx		◊ xxx
	♣ Kxxx		♣ Qxx

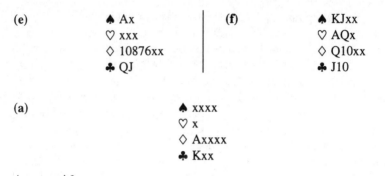

(e)
♠ Ax
♡ xxx
◇ 10876xx
♣ QJ

(f)
♠ KJxx
♡ AQx
◇ Q10xx
♣ J10

(a)
♠ xxxx
♡ x
◇ Axxxx
♣ Kxx

Answer: 4♣

Last time I suggested 5♣ on this hand and that is still a possibility. However, it is my feeling that it will achieve very little other than a silly result. The opposition are almost certain to double you and remember partner's expectation of something like queen to six. Moreover almost everybody has learnt to lead trumps against these sort of sequences now. So, if partner has ♣Qxxxxx, they will be able to lead two rounds of trumps even if they are 2-2. You will then make 5♣ tricks, a heart ruff and the ◇A. Four off for -800 and note that the opposition cannot make a slam. If the trumps are 3-1 they will be able to lead three rounds, you will make no heart ruff and will go for -1100. Yet the opposition still are not guaranteed a slam and they certainly haven't got anywhere near to bidding it yet! With a sound pre-empt opposite we could be certain that 5♣ was going for less than game; with a wild pre-empt opposite it is almost certainly going for more than game. So why bid and give the opposition a free shot? Particularly when they are much more likely to take the money out of wild pre-empts (for exactly this sort of reason). This is simply the first of many examples we will see where I am suggesting that you should bid less opposite a wild pre-empt that opposite a sound one. Surely this is obvious? The more one player pre-empts the less the other must do so in order to avoid getting ridiculously high.

(b)
♠ xx
♡ x
◇ Q987xx
♣ Kxxx

Answer: 5♣

This time I suggest 5♣, the same as last time. Here you know the opposition are cold for game and very probably for a slam. Moreover, you have sufficient support even opposite a wild pre-empt to make 5♣ very likely to be a decent save against game or at worst -800. Queen to six and out should yield you five club tricks and a couple of heart ruffs at least. If you are very much at the wild end of the wild scale and partner turns up with five clubs to the 10 then you will still go for -1100 or so. But now the opposition really seem to be solid for a slam and you have to hope your team-mates bid it.

It is just too restrictive to have to assume partner has 10xxxx for a pre-empt. If that is the case so be it and you have to put up with the result on this hand. Unlike last time, however, to contemplate anything more than 5♣ on this hand is foolish in the extreme. The opposition will certainly double 6♣ and it will go for about the value of their slam. 6♣ is a method of giving the opponents an easy large score against a slam they have not yet bid. It is still worth considering the 'under pre-empt' of 4♣ discussed with this hand last time. It has all the same advantages as before and a couple of extra attractions. You know 4♣ will be a good save against game whereas you cannot be so certain about 5♣. Also, since it is known that you have a wild pre-empting style, then the opposition double you much more freely. Just once in a while you actually end up being doubled in 4♣. It doesn't happen very often but it does occasionally. As always, what is important is to vary your approach on these kind of hands. If you always pre-empt to the limit then everybody knows what you have. Vary it a little and nobody can be quite sure.

(c)   ♠ xxx
                                       ♡ xx
                                       ◇ Axxxx
                                       ♣ Kxx

Answer: Pass

This one is much easier with a wild pre-emptive style than a sound one. You just cannot afford to bid on this hand. 4♣ will go for at least -500 and quite likely -800. Moreover, you are very unlikely to keep them out of game with 4♣. They seem to have plenty of high cards. If they were going to bid game they will anyway. All 4♣ does opposite a random pre-empt is offer the opposition an easier way to an average of about 650 than having to struggle to make game. You should pass like this and hope that the wild pre-empt has already done its job in messing up the opposition. 4♣ is gilding the lily.

(d)
♠ xxx
♡ xxxx
◇ xxx
♣ Qxx

Answer: Pass

You have got to be joking! 3♣ could already be -800 opposite ace to six with the clubs 2-2 and who said partner needs to be that good? Any venture at all by you will just result in a very large minus score. Just pass and let the opposition get on with it. This is really an ideal type of hand to have opposite a wild pre-empt. You hope partner has found a great moment on jack to six (or five?) and out. Now you have really messed up their chance of bidding to their cold grand slam by starting at the three level. Moreover, it is very likely that your pair in the other room will get a free run at it. Pass and hope the wild pre-empt has already done the damage. Bidding something like 5♣ is simply the bid of a sadist who wants to see partner go for about 2000.

(e)
♠ Ax
♡ xxx
◇ 1087xxx
♣ QJ

Answer: Pass

I told you in Chapter 2 I would tell you what happened at the table when this hand came up. At the table the auction went 3♣–Double, and the player bid 4♣ opposite a wild pre-empt. This went responsive double, all pass. After the smoke had cleared the penalty was -1100 opposite

♠ xxx
♡ Kx
◇ xx
♣ 10xxxxx

when the heart finesse was right for declarer but the defence were able to promote the ♣9. Notice of course that the opposition cannot make a slam with the heart finesse correct for you! -1100 was, not surprisingly, -10 IMPs since your team-mates did not attempt the slam. After all they do only have 30 points between them and two balanced hands. Why should they be even looking at a slam? If the heart finesse had been wrong for you then you would have gone for -1400 to gain 1 IMP if your team-mates had bid a slam on a finesse and would lose 12 IMPs if they had stayed out of it. Do you really think this is winning bridge? John Armstrong was around at the time this hand came up (not, I should hasten to add, at the table) and he pointed out the problem very clearly. Either 3♣ or 4♣ is wrong. If your style is to play sound pre-empts then 4♣ is a reasonable shot. But if it is acceptable in your style to open the above hand 3♣, then 4♣ is just silly. The actual outcome is hardly that unlikely and should have been foreseen. The point again is that you cannot be very aggressive in your raises opposite wild pre-empts. You have to hope that the pre-empt has already done its work.

(f)
　　　　　　　　　　　♠ KJxx
　　　　　　　　　　　♡ AQx
　　　　　　　　　　　♢ Q10xx
　　　　　　　　　　　♣ J10

Answer: Pass

Again no other choice. Last time I was suggesting that you could occasionally try a 'cute' 4♣ with this hand. This is bananas opposite a wild pre-empt. The most likely result is that the opposition will just double you and you will go for a silly penalty. Moreover, if the opposition do bid game you have no case at all for doubling it! It could be cold for an overtrick for all you know if partner turns up with ♣Qxxxxx or some other fine collection. This time 4♣ has absolutely no upside at all.

Notice on how many of these hands I have suggested a pass (four out of six). This again is the reverse side of the coin to wild pre-empts. If you pre-empt on wild hands then you cannot afford to raise so freely.

Before I leave the subject of raising partner's wild pre-empts I cannot resisting telling you about a fine coup that I first saw produced by Brian Senior, a player always long on imagination and never afraid of bidding. This coup is particularly useful if you do play wild pre-empts though it can be applicable with sound pre-empts as well. Brian picked up:

　　　　　　　　　　　♠ Qxxx
　　　　　　　　　　　♡ Jxxx
　　　　　　　　　　　♢ –
　　　　　　　　　　　♣ Jxxxx

and heard the auction go:

3 ◇ (i)   Dble(ii)

(i)   Wild
(ii)   Takeout

to him. Now you know what is going to happen, don't you? You know perfectly well that this will go All Pass and 3 ◇ doubled will go for an absolute fortune; it is certainly four figures and could be getting close to -2000 on a really bad day. But what can you do about it? You can hardly redouble for rescue since redouble is generally regarded as a positive manoeuvre here. Even if redouble were rescue, so what? No other suit is likely to play any better and you will just go for a four figure penalty somewhere else. Worse still the opposition may not even make a slam. Partner always holds ace to six when you have a hand like this, and ace and another diamond beats a slam; or maybe your queen make a trick. So you appear to be booked for an awful score and no way out of it. Brian, with remarkable ingenuity, found a way out of it. He raised to 4 ◇ ! so the auction was now:

3 ◇   Dble   4 ◇ (!!)   ??

This had exactly the effect Brian was hoping for. He caught his LHO with ace queen to five diamonds and a 14 count! LHO would dearly have loved to get at 4 ◇ but how do you propose he should go about it? I know of no pair above club standard who do not play responsive doubles in this situation, so he could not double for penalties. To try to get to play 4 ◇ doubled he had to pass and hope partner could re-open with a second double. But that is a really high risk strategy when you have such a good hand. It is unlikely partner will have sufficient values to get another Red card on the table. Moreover, not surprising, the player had to think about this for quite some time, making it even less likely partner would be able to re-open since a slow pass would put ethical constraints on partner and prevent a marginal action from them. The ideal solution to the problem is to bid 3 ♠ and, when you are told this is insufficient, double, thereby silencing partner. Unfortunately, apart from being cheating, the lawmakers have thought of that one (meanies aren't they?) and you are not allowed to change your call to double. So with a sinking heart our man tried Double. Unfortunately his partner knew the system, alerted it and took it out. With one mighty bound Brian was free! Better even than this was to come since in a fit of pique LHO punted 6NT (though it is hard to say what sane call he could have made) and this wandered a couple off in the fullness of time.

So Brian had managed to turn -1400 into +200. Quite a coup. Yet once you have the imagination to think of the call (it would never have occurred to a simpleton like me) it is clearly the correct thing to do. What are you risking? The very worst thing that can happen is that you play in 4 ◊ doubled rather than 3 ◊ doubled. Provided that you have a sympathetic partner (sympathetic in this context is defined as someone who does not blow your head off as soon as they see the dummy), this will simply go one more off (indeed, it might even get out for the same score since the opposition will be so busy laughing at you that they might drop a trick). This might matter in aggregate but the IMP or matchpoint difference between -1400 and -1700 is virtually zero. Hence you have everything to gain by trying this manoeuvre and only a couple of IMPs to lose by risking the extra 300. (I was once playing in a team with Richard Fleet. I made a particularly silly vulnerable pre-empt, got doubled and was booked for -1100. The defence went slightly astray and I was given an option where I could settle for -1100 or try for -800 but at the risk of going for -1400. Applying the above reasoning that there is very little difference between -1100 and -1400 I went for the -800 option and it worked. As it happened they had made the same daft call in the other room and Richard had not mis-defended it so it had gone for -1100. Richard informed me that if I had brought back -1400 on this board he would have told me clearly and distinctly what the difference between -1100 and -1400 was. Do you know, I believe him!)

On the hand above Brian used the opposition's methods (which after all were standard methods) to get himself out of a jam. This idea of using the opposition's agreements is applicable in a surprisingly large number of situations. However, you have to be aware of the possibility and have the flexibility of mind to think of the problem from the opponents' point of view as well as your own. The following hand has nothing to do with pre-empts but consider this bidding problem from one of the magazines a couple of years ago:

♠ KQ10xx
♡ x
◊ x
♣ KQxxxx

| 1NT | Dble | ? |

Now this really is a revolting problem. Without the double we could have got out our transfers and bid the hand happily. But without a lot of methods you cannot do that any more. Anyone who passes or redoubles (I had 10 points, partner!) is being rather naive. It seems all too likely that RHO has a nice juicy red suit to run so that is out of the question. 2NT as an artificial game force is a possibility but do you really want to force to game and anyway will you be able to get both of your suits in? If 4♡ for example from RHO comes back to you, you are really stuffed; 4♠, 5♣, Pass or Double could all be right and you have no idea which. So is there a solution? There was a large vote amongst the expert panel for a quiet 2♣. Whilst this may seem exceptionally timid it is hardly likely that 2♣ is going to get passed out when you have two red singletons, is it? However, that is not the point. The point is that almost every pair play that the sequence:

1NT   Dble   2♣/2♢

is *forcing* on them. Thus one of the opponents has to bid and you will then get a chance to introduce your spade suit. You have thus got in both suits and have shown the relative lengths with absolutely no risks. Clever, isn't it? And possible all because you have used the opposition's extremely sensible agreements to your advantage. All you need in this sort of situation is a basic knowledge of the oppositions methods and the flexibility to think of what the opposition must then do and how you can use it to your advantage.

OK, enough of the digression. Let's move onto the hands on which we introduced a new suit. Remember we are playing non-forcing responses.

(a)
♠ AKx
♡ KQJxxx
♢ xx
♣ Ax

(b)
♠ AK
♡ AKQJxxxx
♢ xx
♣ A

(c)
♠ KQJxxx
♡ AKQxx
♢ xx
♣ –

(d)
♠ AJ10xxxx
♡ x
♢ Axx
♣ xx

(e)
♠ AKxx
♡ xx
♢ AQxx
♣ AJx

(f)
♠ AKxx
♡ AQx
♢ xx
♣ AJxx

(g)   ♠ AQJx   (h)   ♠ Axxx
             ♡ xxx   ♡ xx
             ◊ xx   ◊ xxx
             ♣ Qxxx   ♣ Kxxx?

(a)   ♠ AKx
                         ♡ KQJxxx
                         ◊ xx
                         ♣ Ax

Answer: 3♡

Just as last time we bid 3♡. Again just like last time this could well be the
wrong thing to do: we could well be turning a plus score into a negative
one. However, as before, 4♡ could be excellent, so we should give it a go.
Strangely it is more clear cut to bid 3♡ on this hand opposite a wild pre-
empt than a sound one.

Firstly, you could actually be turning a negative score into a positive one
rather than the other way round (!) when partner passes 3♡, which makes
and 3♣ does not (it is easy to see a heart, two diamonds and a couple of
trump losers in 3♣ opposite a wild pre-empt for example).

Secondly, the shorter partner is allowed to be in clubs the more likelihood
that partner has some heart support. Hence the chance of a heart fit is
increased opposite a wild pre-empt. Together these two make 3♡ clear cut
on the hand.

(b)   ♠ AK
                         ♡ AKQJxxxx
                         ◊ xx
                         ♣ A

Answer: 4♡

Thank you, partner! And thank you, methods! Opposite a wild pre-empt
you have no idea at all what is in partner's hand and since you are playing
change of suit as non-forcing you cannot possibly find out. Hence you
have no choice. There may be a slam on but you have no possible way of
finding out. You have to follow Skid Simon's dictum and take:

   '*the best result possible rather than the best possible result.*'

Skid was actually talking about winning at rubber bridge opposite a very poor partner, but perhaps it is just as much in context here. You have no choice but to shrug your shoulders and bid 4♡, knowing that that will be the correct contract 99% of the time and resigning yourself to missing the slam the other 1%.

(c)   ♠ KQJxxx
                                          ♡ AKQxx
                                          ◇ xx
                                          ♣ –

Answer: 3♠

Yes, I know it is non-forcing and partner might well pass with game on. If you feel like it go ahead and bid 4♠. That is a reasonable shot but in my opinion unnecessary and fairly random. A lot of the time when you can make 4♠ partner will have a go at it over 3♠. Don't forget that at the moment you have ♠A and ◇AK off the top and you still have to do something with the hearts. Partner is thus going to need a couple of spades at least and either a ruffing value in hearts or a diamond trick. Quite a lot to hope for if you punt 4♠. If you do, partner is just as likely to put down a singleton or void and it will have no play at all. You might well be doubled in 4♠ as well.

Thus I would just hope to improve the contract by bidding 3♠ and hope it makes with an outside chance that partner will bid 4♠. How do you get to hearts? You don't unless partner drums up another bid. In these methods it is impossible. You have to resign yourself to playing in 3♠ or 4♠. If 4♡ was the correct contract that is simply tough.

Those who live by the sword …

(d)   ♠ AJ10xxxx
                                          ♡ x
                                          ◇ Axx
                                          ♣ xx

Answer: 3♠

A great hand for a non-forcing 3♠. A good job really after the last two disasters for it. Bid a non-forcing 3♠ and await partner's reaction. If partner raises to four, great and if partner passes, 3♠ will very likely make more tricks than 3♣ with a wild pre-empt opposite. I know players who would bid 4♠ on that hand, arguing that opposite a wild pre-empt the opposition are very likely to be cold for 4♡ and you should get to 4♠ as fast as possible. There is a lot to be said for this and I do not mind 4♠. However, if partner has support, partner will raise if the opposition bid 4♡ and if not you do not really want to take the save. You might even beat 4♡ if partner has a singleton spade.

(e)   ♠ AKxx
                             ♡ xx
                             ◇ AQxx
                             ♣ AJx

Answer: Pass

We are now getting to the kind of hands that really decide what your bottom limit for a wild pre-empt is. It may seem ridiculous to pass such a good hand with seemingly such a good chance of 3NT. But just think about this.

How wild is your style of pre-empting? If your style of pre-empt is such that partner is always expected to open 3♣ at Green on queen to six or 10 to six or queen to five or even five small then you cannot afford to bid on hand (e). That will be turning a very likely plus score into a negative score in search of a Holy Grail of 3NT. However, if your pre-empts are not quite that wild then it is sensible to move forward. King to six and the ♡K for example will make 3NT simply dependent on the club suit coming in (a 52% shot) and hence make it a very acceptable contract.

But this brings us on to the next problem: what are you going to bid? Last time I suggested 3◇ but now that is non-forcing and you could end up playing in a very embarrassing 4-1 fit. Thus if you are going to bid you have to just shut your eyes and bid 3NT. This may be the correct thing to do but it is pretty unlikely. Partner will need a heart stop; you will be playing it the wrong way round anyway with the lead coming through partner's stop; and there is absolutely no guarantee that partner's club suit will come in opposite such 'feeble' support as AJx. Even if you change our methods and bid a forcing 3◇, then there is no guarantee you will end up in the correct place. If partner bids 3♡ you have to bid 3NT and you still have the same concern about partner's club suit. If partner doesn't bid 3♡ you will have to subside in 4♣ with no guarantee that that will make. Give partner:

♠ xxx
♡ xx
◇ xx
♣ Qxxxxx

and you need both minor suit finesses to make 4♣ and plenty of helicopters to get to his hand to take them. Last time I blithely said that, if partner does not have a heart stop, you 'can bid 5♣ in the sure knowledge that it is a decent contract'. Now it is likely to vary from awful to no play at all, so it cannot seriously be considered.

It is true that 5♣ could be very good even opposite a wild pre-empt. For example:

♠ xxx
♡ x
◇ xx
♣ K109xxxx

would open 3♣ in a wild style quite happily and now 5♣ is on the diamond finesse with the chance of a 3-3 spade break if they do not force you to take it. Why then am I suggesting that you pass when either of two games might be good? The point is that you have no idea what the correct thing to do is and no way of finding out. Sometimes you can make 3NT; sometimes you can make 5♣; sometimes you cannot even make 3♣ and 4♣ will often be too high. Thus playing a very wild pre-empting style you just have to pass this hand.

This may seem pretty random. That is because it is pretty random. It is the nature of the beast; random bids produce random results. The hope is that more of these results will be in your favour than against you. By the way you should get used to passing wild pre-empts with these hands in tempo, without a flicker that you have anything to think about. Every so often you catch LHO with a reasonable hand and they protect! Then you suddenly have a big upside again. Sit and agonise over what to do for 10 minutes and nobody is going to protect on a marginal hand.

(f)   ♠ AKxx
                            ♡ AQx
                            ◇ xx
                            ♣ AJxx

Answer: 3NT

OK, this time the fourth club has swayed me. Even I cannot bear to pass on AK, A and AJ to four clubs. Though I know people who would and again it could be the correct thing to do. It just seems protecting yourself against a very weak pre-empt too much. So what to bid? The problem is that unless you have agreed to play new suits as forcing then 3♡ is out. So you basically have a choice between 3NT and 5♣ since if you are going to bid you might as well have a shot at the game bonus. 3NT may seem silly with ◇xx but 5♣ will be just as silly if partner has ◇Qxxx and ♣10xxxxx.

The choice here really depends on how wild wild can be. If partner is allowed to hold five small then bidding 5♣ is ridiculous, whereas partner may have enough diamonds to protect you from that attack. Again the fewer cards partner is allowed to have in their suit the more cards they will have outside. If partner's worst holding is ♣Q10xxxx then 5♣ becomes much more attractive as a possibility. Hence I shut my eyes and bid 3NT. It will either make or be a very silly contract. That will not be much different from most of my contracts.

(g)   ♠ AQJx
                                ♡ xxx
                                ◇ xx
                                ♣ Qxxx

Answer: 3♠

Here I have a considerable liking for a non-forcing 3♠ bid. In this case it is not meant as an attempt to improve the contract nor as a game try but simply as a lead-directional bid. You certainly want a spade lead against whatever contract they will be in so why not try and get one. What can go wrong? You get passed out in 3♠? Great! You go for a few 50s. Partner raises you? Still fine as long as you are not doubled and if you are you can retreat to 5♣, knowing that at least you have a double fit and 5♣ is now quite likely to be a good save. You could bid 5♣ straight away and that is certainly reasonable. But you have to accept that they will certainly double you and unlike over a sound pre-empt where it was very likely to be a good save here it is certain to be -500 and very likely to be -800. 4♣ seems to achieve absolutely nothing that 3♠ does not and does not have its lead-directing quality, so I would not recommend that. The choice is thus between a lead-directing 3♠ and an aggressive 5♣, hoping that they misjudge at the five level.

(h)
        ♠ Axxx
        ♡ xx
        ◇ xxx
        ♣ Kxxx

Answer: 4♣ or 5♣

Here bidding 3♠ seems just silly. You do not want a spade lead, indeed on a number of layouts with a minor honour in partner's hand it could be disastrous. So the options seem to be passing or raising clubs. Pass seems awfully wet even opposite a random pre-empt, so that leaves 4♣ or 5♣. Which you choose is really a function of the partnership philosophy, your temperament, perhaps more importantly your partner's temperament (they will have to play it, after all), and the opposition.

If the partnership is happy to go for a likely -800 and a possible -1100 in order to force a high-level guess on the opposition, then bid 5♣. Maybe more relevantly, if you know the opposition like to bid over pre-empts, then you should try 5♣. If on the other hand partner gets ratty at going for what they think is a silly -1100 ('you knew I would have queen to six and nothing') then 5♣ is daft. It is even sillier if you know the opposition like to defend pre-empts. Anyone who bids 5♣ on this hand against Helme-Bowyer for example wants their bumps feeling. A red card will appear from both sides of the table before anyone has bothered to look at their hand. Personally I would go with 4♣ – but then I always was lily-livered.

Finally, how about responding to wild major suit pre-empts? When discussing sound pre-empts I said that it was much easier to respond to major suit pre-empts than minor suit ones since you now had the easy option of playing game in partner's major, knowing this will be a sensible contract. Regrettably this is no longer the case and responding to wild major suit pre-empts is even more of a pain than responding to wild minor suit pre-empts for the simple reason that you have even less room than before. You cannot be so certain about strain and will often have to think about alternative possibilities.

There is also a school of thought that allows major suit pre-empts to be wilder than minor suit ones. Basically, if you choose to play wild pre-empts there are three possible styles:

(i) All three level pre-empts are wild.

The argument here is that, if you believe in disrupting the opponents with wild pre-empts, then it should make little difference whether you pick up a bad hand with a six (five?) card major or a six (five?) card minor. Either way you want to cause the opponents some pain.

(ii) Only the minor suit pre-empts are wild; the majors are rather sounder.

This is perhaps the least popular of the available styles, though I have seen it played. The idea here is that partner needs so much more to make game over a minor suit pre-empt (particularly if the suit can be a little less than classical) that they do over a major suit pre-empt. Hence partner will sometimes bid game over a major pre-empt on the off chance that you occasionally have something. Thus to avoid playing in suits, such as six small opposite queen-one with a couple of outside losers, it is decided that major suit pre-empts should be of reasonable quality.

(iii) Only the major suit pre-empts are wild; the minor are rather sounder.

Whilst almost unknown in Britain it is a reasonably popular style in the States. The idea is that minor suit pre-empts are not the greatest destructive tool in the universe. They leave the entire three level available to the opposition and in particular both majors. So, if you wildly pre-empt minors you are not causing as much grief as you might hope to the opposition whilst at the same time ruining your own constructive game chances. Hence some pairs have a rule that minor suit pre-empts first or second in hand (as usual third in hand anything goes) should be at least KQxxxx.

On the other hand major suit pre-empts, and particularly 3♠, do cause a headache to the opposition in that they take away the entire three level and force the opposition to choose 3NT or another game contract immediately. Hence major suit pre-empts are allowed to be very wild. Some pairs attempt to have their cake and eat it by playing sound minor suit pre-empts and then having a conventional bid to show wild minor suit pre-empts.

Let's look at the same hands as last time, assuming that partner has opened 3♠ at Green in a wild style. We will look at them in the same order, that is, potential 3NT hands, raises, and new suits. By the way, even playing wild pre-empts it is normal to play 4♣ or 4♦ over three of a major as forcing. It is a very rare hand that partner wants to try and stop on a pinhead in four of a minor. If you really do have a void spade and ♦KQ10xxxxx either pass and take your bumps or try increasing the pre-empt with 5♦ which might be very effective. Even a forcing 4♦ could work very well. It will tell partner where your values are if nothing else.

(a)   ♠ Axx   **(c)**   ♠ Jx
    ♡ KQxxx   ♡ AQxx
    ◊ Ax   ◊ AKJx
    ♣ Axx   ♣ KQx

(b)   ♠ x
    ♡ Kx
    ◊ AKQJxxx
    ♣ Axx

(a)   ♠ Axx
    ♡ KQxxx
    ◊ Ax
    ♣ Axx

Answer: Pass

It is now very unlikely that 3NT will have any play at all since partner's suit is not likely to come in for no losers. It is also entirely possible that 4♠ will not make. Give partner a hand such as:

    ♠ QJxxxx
    ♡ x
    ◊ xxx
    ♣ xxx

and 4♠ has very little play on a minor suit lead. Moreover partner need not be that good though it is true that they could be rather more suitable. Thus pass has to be considered a very sensible option. However, partner could have a very useful hand such as:

    ♠ KQxxxx
    ♡ xx
    ◊ xxx
    ♣ xx

making 4♠ excellent. You just have to bid 4♠ and hope partner is suitable.

(b)

♠ x
♡ Kx
◊ AKQJxxx
♣ Axx

Answer: 3NT

The second hand is still a clear 3NT call. You have a reasonable shot at making 3NT with a little help from partner and certainly should not go more than one off. 4♠ on the other hand is just silly; you could easily be playing queen to six opposite a singleton with an outside ace off the contract.

(c)

♠ Jx
♡ AQxx
◊ AKJx
♣ KQx

Answer: 4♠

The third hand is the most problematical. And it again depends on just how wild your pre-empts can be. I would raise to 4♠ and hope to get away with two trump losers and the ♣A. However, you can easily construct hands where 3NT is actually correct (or 'horror of horrors' no game makes). For example:

♠ Qxxxxx
♡ Jx
◊ x
♣ J10xx

gives 4♠ almost no play whereas you at least have a shot at 3NT if you can reach the dummy with the ♡J at an appropriate time. So opposite a wild 3♠ the choice between 3NT and 4♠ is much closer.

How about raising partner?

(a)	♠ Kxx ♡ x ◊ Axxxx ♣ xxxx		**(c)**	♠ Kxx ♡ xx ◊ Axxxx ♣ xxx
(b)	♠ Kxxx ♡ x ◊ Q987xx ♣ xx		**(d)**	♠ Qxx ♡ xxxx ◊ xxx ♣ xxx

(e)	♠ QJ	(f)	♠ J10
	♡ xxx		♡ AQx
	◇ 1087xxx		◇ Q10xx
	♣ Ax		♣ KJxx

Of these:

(a) Is a clear 4♠.

(b) Can also bid 4♠. However, even opposite a wild pre-empt, 5♠ would appear to be a lot more sensible as an attempt to give the opposition a problem and that would be my choice. 6♠ just seems too much of a good thing.

(c) Is a 4♠ bid but it is far less clear than it was last time. True the opposition will make game but it is not likely that they will make a slam. Moreover it is very likely that 4♠ will go for at least -800, more than their game. If we give partner our frequently used standard example of:

♠ QJxxxx
♡ x
◇ xxx
♣ xxx

then this is -800 without the option and the opposition will have to bid and make a slam to beat that score. Reverse partner's red suits and the diamond ruff will beat any slam and if the trumps are 3-1 then trump leads will still take 4♠ for -800. Since the opposition are very likely to double 4♠ rather than bid at the five level, 4♠ on this hand is not as obvious as it might at first appear. It is probably still worth doing though for the extra problems it may cause the opposition. After all, the opposition do not always do the right thing. If they did there would be very little point in pre-empting.

(d) I would pass on hand (d). 4♠ is a possibility but it just seems too risky. You cannot really expect more than five spade tricks as your total and that gives -1100. Anything worse than that and they will not have to bid a slam at all. Pass and hope the wild pre-empt has already done its job.

(e) Is a clear-cut pass for exactly the reasons I discussed with this hand over a 3♣ pre-empt. To bid 4♠ is just to go for a large penalty for no good reason at all. Pass and hope 3♠ has done the job.

(f) Is a clear pass. 3♠ is unlikely to have any play and the opposition can possibly make very little. This is the kind of hand you hate to hold opposite a wild pre-empt: enough high cards to make it unlikely the opposition can bid game; enough defence to possibly beat it if they do; and not enough to give partner much of a chance in 3♠. You are likely to get a small minus score where a less wild style might have resulted in a small plus score.

Finally, introducing a new suit.

(a)
♠ Ax
♡ KQJxxx
◇ xx
♣ AKx

(e)
♠ AJx
♡ xx
◇ AQxx
♣ AKxx

(b)
♠ A
♡ AKQJxxxx
◇ xx
♣ AK

(f)
♠ AJxx
♡ AQx
◇ xx
♣ AKxx

(c)
♠ –
♡ AKQxx
◇ xx
♣ KQJxxx

(g)
♠ Qxxx
♡ xxx
◇ xx
♣ AQJx

(d)
♠ xx
♡ x
◇ Axx
♣ AJ10xxxx

(h)
♠ Axxx
♡ xx
◇ xxx
♣ Kxxx

(a)
♠ Ax
♡ KQJxxx
◇ xx
♣ AKx

Answer: 4♡

This really is nowhere near as easy as before. Last time I suggested raising to 4♠ as a clear-cut action. Here that is far from so. Opposite a wild pre-empt 4♡ could be much better than 4♠. Indeed there could be no game on at all and it could be correct to pass, though that seems a somewhat extreme position. Your choice of game depends largely on just how wild your style is. If partner will never have less than queen to six then clearly 4♠ is the obvious call. On the other hand if partner could have six small, or worse jack to five, for the pre-empt, then 4♠ is pretty silly and you should try 4♡. Remember again that the fewer cards partner is systemically allowed to have in the pre-empt suit the more cards they will, on average, provide for your suit. The only downside of this argument is that partner will be more inclined to a wild pre-empt if they are worried about the ♡ suit than anything else. Thus they may well find 3♠ (if it is allowed in your style) on:

♠ xxxxxx
♡ x
◇ xxx
♣ Qxx

when 4♡ has absolutely no play at all, but not on:

♠ xxxxxx
♡ xxx
◇ x
♣ Qxx

when 4♡ is almost cold. Notice by the way how strong the argument for pass is. I have very kindly given partner a highly valuable ♣Q and a highly valuable diamond singleton. Reverse the minors in the second hand and 4♡ still has absolutely no play despite three trumps and singleton opposite. Perhaps then Pass is the correct answer but I am sure very few players would do so simply because they could not stand the tension of waiting to find out. One strong argument for bidding is that 4♡ may simply make more tricks than 3♠ if partner has a very wild pre-empt. In the first hand above 3♠ is one down if the trumps break and more if not, whereas 4♡ is only one off if the trumps break. In the second hand 3♠ needs the spade break and no heart ruffs to make, whereas 4♡ is virtually cold.

Thus bidding 4♡ does have the advantage that it is likely to make as many tricks as 3♠ does and at least achieve a game bonus if it makes.

(b)   ♠ A
                          ♡ AKQJxxxx
                          ◇ xx
                          ♣ AK

Answer: 4♡

An easy one. 4♡ is surely clear cut for exactly the kind of reasons discussed with this hand after a 3♣ pre-empt. Yes, you may make six but you probably will not. No bid will find out what you want to know so give it up and take the money.

(c)
$\spadesuit$ –
$\heartsuit$ AKQxx
$\diamondsuit$ xx
$\clubsuit$ KQJxxxx

Answer: 4$\heartsuit$

Thanks again, partner!

Last time I suggested pass with this hand opposite a sound pre-empt. Here that just does not seem like a sensible option to me. Opposite a wild pre-empt 3$\spadesuit$ could possibly be off in trump tricks! Certainly it will have no play for less than two or three off so you might as well try and improve the contract. You could try 4$\clubsuit$ if that is non-forcing in your repertoire but otherwise you are pretty much left with 4$\heartsuit$. You do not really expect 4$\heartsuit$ to make (though it might) but it will almost certainly make more tricks than 3$\spadesuit$. There is no point passing 3$\spadesuit$ and hoping somebody protects by the way. This seems very unlikely to me. The opposition will have too many spades(!) and not enough hearts to seriously consider a protection.

(d)
$\spadesuit$ xx
$\heartsuit$ x
$\diamondsuit$ Axx
$\clubsuit$ AJ10xxxx

Answer: 4$\spadesuit$

The same action as suggested last time. You will certainly have no play for this and indeed it could be very expensive if the opposition are able to draw two rounds of trumps and cash out their heart tricks.

However, it does seem a little wet to pass when the opposition as so likely to have 4$\heartsuit$ on. You may get away with this undoubled if you bid it confidently and quickly enough. Otherwise you will have to hope that it is -500 or -800 at worst. The only other possibilities are Pass and 4$\clubsuit$. 4$\clubsuit$ is, as before, lead-directional in nature but it seems to me to have even less merit than before. If you bid 4$\clubsuit$ you are committed to passing out 4$\heartsuit$ since your opponents will now certainly double 4$\spadesuit$ for a decent score. So bidding 4$\clubsuit$ is betting on your chances to beat 4$\heartsuit$, which seems long odds against opposite a wild pre-empt. Pass is to hope that the wild pre-empt has already done the damage to the opposition and that raising to 4$\spadesuit$ is unnecessary. This is certainly the safer option but if you play wild pre-empts safety is not normally a primary consideration.

(e)
♠ AJx
♡ xx
◇ AQxx
♣ AKxx

Answer: 4♠

An easy one. Bid 4♠ and hope it makes! 4♠ is not guaranteed opposite a wild pre-empt but it is clearly downright silly to do anything else. Even a real dog from partner such as:

♠ xxxxxx
♡ xxx
◇ xx
♣ xx

will make 4♠ if the spades are 2-2 and the diamond finesse is working. Not much of a contract I know but anything better from partner will improve your chances.

(f)
♠ AJxx
♡ AQx
◇ xx
♣ AKxx

Answer: 4♠

As above. 4♠ is now even more obvious since the fourth trump will bolster even the most suspect of pre-empt suits.

(g)
♠ Qxxx
♡ xxx
◇ xx
♣ AQJx

Answer: 4♠

As in the discussion of this hand under sound pre-empts don't even think of anything else! Bid 4♠ and let them get on with it. Your expectation in 4♠ is about three off but that is still a save against game and it may be better than that (you are a little unlucky if it is a lot worse than that; your club values being useless for example). Again you can try a clever 4♣ if you want when your suit is hearts but not when it is spades. Take away the four level as fast as you can.

(h)
                              ♠ Axxx
                              ♡ xx
                              ◊ xxx
                              ♣ Kxxx

Answer: 4♠

As above. You could occasionally try 4♡ just to keep the opposition awake but it is not something to be tried on a regular basis. Apart from trips to the Laws and Ethics Committee the opposition usually pick up this sort of adventure and it simply serves to give them more room.

Responding to Random Pre-empts

We have so far looked at how to respond to both sound and wild pre-empts and to pre-empts in all positions and vulnerabilities. The very last item to look at is what to do opposite a random style of pre-empting.

I wish I had some sensible advice to offer you but I don't!

If you genuinely play random pre-empts where a three level opening can be anything from six small and a bust to king jack to seven and an outside king, then I have no idea how you can bid sensibly over them. Of course, this is why thoroughly random pre-empts are fairly unpopular. Constructive bidding over them is completely impossible, far more so than over a wild pre-empt when at least you know what partner has got (or more accurately what he has not got!).

The adherents of random pre-empts maintain that it is important to pre-empt as often as possible and therefore both bad and good pre-empts should be included. It is also more difficult for the opponents to defend and bid if they do not know if the pre-empt is weak or strong. 'A pre-empt that is always known to be weak is a blunt tool,' to quote Reese again.

There are two opponents and only one partner and hence you have a two to one shot of hitting an opponent with the problem and not partner. All this is entirely true but that does not reduce the headache when the idiot opposite opens a random pre-empt and you have a good hand.

About the only thing you can do is assume partner has a middling hand for the range. So if a non-vulnerable pre-empt can be anything from six small to king-jack to seven then assume a six card suit (since six card suits are more common than seven card suits) and assume an honour (since one honour in a six card suit is about average). So bid on the assumption that partner has about king to six. If you can see chances of game opposite that, bid, otherwise pass. If partner has a lot better hand than that you will miss some good games and if partner has a lot worse hand than that you will bid a lot of silly ones. But that is the nature of the style. Random bids produce random results.

It is also a matter of partnership discussion whether new suits should be played as forcing or non-forcing over random pre-empts. There are arguments on both sides but maybe it is sensible that they should be forcing. That at least gives partner a chance to describe the nature of their pre-empt and does not force a good hand opposite to guess the final contract immediately. On the other hand non-forcing responses allow responder to introduce a decent suit which can be passed or raised depending on how good or bad the pre-empt was. Partnerships will need to sort this out for themselves.

4
THE NATURAL
WEAK TWO BID

Question: How many psychotherapists does it take to change a light bulb?

Answer: One, but only if the light bulb really wants to change.

Question: What on earth has that got to do with Bridge?

Answer: Nothing. I just thought after the last two chapters you might like a break.

So, back to work. On the market today, available at all reputable stores, are a plethora of various conventions for all two level openings, ranging from constructive to highly destructive and from straightforward to downright weird. Most of these saw their heyday in the eighties when there was an explosion of both constructive and destructive bidding theory. Recently there has been something of a backlash against artificial pre-empts and openings. I will discuss the reasons for this later on. Today it is very common to find expert pairs playing entirely natural weak twos in the majors. It is a peculiarly English variation I think that a number of top pairs also play 2◇ as a natural weak two. 2◇ has had a long and varied history as bridge bidding has changed. Twenty years ago in *Bridge Conventions, Finesses and Coups* Terence Reese wrote:

> 'Unnecessary as a strong bid, ineffective as a weak bid, 2◇ has become the play thing of modern theorists.'

If this was true twenty years ago it was even more the case after that as convention after convention made use of 2◇. Now there is a body of opinion that returns it to a natural weak call. How strange.

In this chapter I shall concentrate on the natural weak two bid, particularly 2♠ and 2♡ which are very widely played but also taking into account the weak 2◇ as well. Assuming that you are playing weak two bids, what then should you open a weak two on? It will not surprise you to know that my answer to this question is the same as to what you should open a three level pre-empt on. It depends. And it depends on all the same items that the choice for a three level opening depended upon. That is, offence to defence ratio, vulnerability, position at the table, state of the match and partnership philosophy.

I have no intention of going through all the ramifications of the effects of vulnerability and position at the table again. The arguments are exactly the same as they were at the three level. I am sure that by now you are bored to tears with such discussions and those of you who are not are asleep. So I will confine myself to the effect of partnership philosophy on weak twos.

What you open a weak two on depends on what you consider sensible for a three level opening. If you regard AQ to seven as normal even for a non-vulnerable pre-empt then it makes sense that your weak twos should be AQ to six or thereabouts. On the other hand if you believe in wild pre-empts and regard king to six perfectly adequate, then what are you going to open weak twos on? Presumably something weaker. In Britain the standard method of playing weak twos is to open weak twos on one less card than you would weak three bids. So if you regard seven card suits as normal for three openers then six card suits are normal for two openers. If six card suits are normal for your three bids then five card suits are regarded as normal for weak two bids. Note that this needs to be on the convention card. Without other information opponents are entitled to assume that a weak two bid shows six card suits, so if you regularly open five card suits then this needs to be specified. If you allow six card non-vulnerable three bids but expect seven for a vulnerable three bid, then again five card weak twos non-vulnerable and six card weak twos vulnerable would be normal.

Before we go on to a fuller discussion of the effect of partnership style on weak two openings it is worth noting that, whilst the above is the standard British method, it is not the only method played. There is a style played by a number of partnerships in America which allows very wild three openers but insists on highly disciplined two openers. In this style a non-vulnerable 3 ♠ is perfectly acceptable on:

♠ 10xxxxx
♡ xx
◇ xxxx
♣ x

but for a non-vulnerable 2 ♠ a hand such as:

♠ AQJxxx
♡ xx
♦ xxxx
♣ x

is expected. This looks positively weird to English eyes but there is method behind the apparent madness. The argument is that as random destructive weapons weak two bids are not very effective. Everybody can cope with them effectively and the opponents have plenty of room to sort out their combined assets. Hence it is not the most efficient use of a weak two bid to have it as a wild destructive weapon. Instead, argue the proponents of this style, you should use it as a constructive aid to your own bidding. You should use a weak two bid to show a decent six card suit in a hand less than an opening bid. Over this you can then make aggressive game tries (usually with some artificial machinery to help) and may be able to bid good minimum point count games (either 3NT or 4♡/4♠ as appropriate). Here you are using the relatively low level of the weak two as a positive aid to your own constructive bidding. On the other hand, the three level is still very effective as a destructive attack on the opponents communications. Hence three level pre-empts are opened as often as possible and become very wild. Rather perversely a lot of hands that would be regarded as normal non-vulnerable pre-empts in this country, such as AQJ to six, are opened at the two level in this style.

Give it a try if you feel like it and see how it works. However, for the rest of this chapter I shall concentrate on the standard British method. That is, I shall assume that the strength of our weak twos is directly related to the strength of our three bids; the sounder the three opener, the sounder the weak two and vice versa.

Weak Two Bids in a Sound Style

Let's start by examining what a weak two might look like playing a sound style. We'll start the discussion by looking at a first in hand non-vulnerable weak two. As with all pre-empts a key factor is your offence to defence ratio. Ideally for a pre-empt you want a high offensive strength together with a poor (in a perfect world non-existent) defensive strength. Many pairs play a nominal point count for their weak twos, 5-9 being the most popular, but this is really a pretty meaningless piece of data since the hand texture and honour distribution are much more relevant that the overall point count. Thus:

♠ Jxxxxx
♡ Ax
◇ xxx
♣ Ax

is a truly dreadful example of a weak two and no expert player of my acquaintance would dream of opening 2♠ on this hand (though many would open 1♠). You have a very poor suit, the worst distribution for a hand with a six card suit in it and stacks of defence (how can partner possibly credit you with two outside aces for a weak two opening?). If you get doubled in 2♠ you are likely to be going sailing when the opposition can make nothing beyond a part score because of all your defence. Add to this that you do not particularly want a spade lead if the opponents play the contract. You would be much happier if partner were to lead their own suit of hearts or clubs against no trumps, for example. The last thing you want to see is partner producing the ♠K from ♠Kx against any contract by the opposition. Anyone who opens 2♠ on this hand because 'It was in the range, partner' is a dedicated point-counter of the worst sort. Contrast this with:

♠ KJ109xx
♡ xx
◇ xxx
♣ xx

which is a great example of a 2♠ opening. Here you have good offence (you would be very unlucky not to be able to take four tricks in spades even if partner puts down nothing at all) and no defence at all. If partner puts down nothing for you in 2♠ doubled then you will go for -800 but the opponents are very likely to make a slam. On the previous hand you could be going for -1100 or even -1400 in 2♠ doubled and yet you know that the opponents cannot make a slam because of your aces. Finally you really want a spade lead from partner. Moreover, no honours in partner's hand can be damaged by the spade lead; if partner chooses to lead from ♠Qx or ♠Ax then that is fine by you. This hand is a fine example of a weak 2♠ and again anyone who would not open it because 'It was not in the range' is simply counting points and not looking at the hand as a whole. Expanding on this, I also think that:

♠ QJ109xx
♡ xx
◇ xxx
♣ xx

is a 2♠ opening bid whereas:

♠ 10xxxxx
♡ KQ
◇ QJ10
♣ xx

is not, for all the reasons discussed above. See what I mean about announcing a point range for a weak two as being rather irrelevant? At best it is a rough guide as to your pre-emptive style but I have the feeling that it would be much more sensible to have pairs specify how wild the weak two might be, including how weak the suit may be and the minimum number of cards possible.

It is worth pointing out that many pairs would regard the second hand:

♠ KJ109xx
♡ xx
◇ xxx
♣ xx

as too strong for a non-vulnerable weak two. For players who have a wild pre-emptive style this is a routine 3♠ opening. To be fair, even in a sound style this hand is close in my opinion. Provided you allow three level pre-empts on six card suits then this hand has a lot to recommend it, particularly the quality of the suit and the lack of any outside strength. Personally I would not open this one at the three level. However, change the hand to:

♠ KJ109xx
♡ x
◇ xxxx
♣ xx

and make sure the vulnerability is Green (rather than just non-vulnerable) and I would probably open 3♠ first in hand, would definitely open 2♠ second in hand and would consider 3♠ routine third in hand. Before you ask, yes, I would pass fourth in hand. Fifteen years ago this would have been regarded as a minimum weak two, now it is a middle-of-the-road three opener for many pairs.

It is also worth pointing out that some players do not agree with my views on offence to defence ratio for weak twos and particularly on my views about suit quality. Many players who do not regard themselves as particularly wild pre-emptors believe it is simply winning tactics to open weak twos on almost all sub opening bid hands containing six card suits. So they would be quite happy to open a weak two on jack to six with a couple of kings outside. To be fair, I do not mind opening weak twos on poorish suits either, I just do not want to have too much defence outside. Thus I would be quite happy to open 2♠ on:

♠ J10xxxx
♡ xx
◇ KJxx
♣ x

where I have poor defence outside and some extra offence in the form of a decent diamond suit. Notice again that in a wild pre-emptive style many players would consider this normal for a non-vulnerable 3♠. I would also be quite happy to open 2♠ on:

♠ Q10xxxx
♡ Qxx
◇ Jxx
♣ x

Here you have very little defence to anything and. whilst this could go horribly wrong if you are doubled and partner puts down enough bits and pieces to prevent them making anything, it does seem a bit wet to pass this hand. On the other hand I would not open 2♠ on:

♠ Jxxxxx
♡ Ax
◇ Kxxx
♣ x

nor on:

♠ Jxxxxx
♡ KQxx
◇ xx
♣ x

Many players, however, would open 2♠ on both of these hands (though nobody I know will open a weak two with two outside aces). I wouldn't open these hands for the following reasons. In the first example you have too much defence and too much offence; in other words, the hand is too strong despite the low point count. The second example is a real exercise in trying to shoot yourself in the foot. You have a lousy spade suit and an excellent four card heart suit. What are you trying to achieve? The most likely results of opening 2♠ on this hand is that either you will keep the opponents out of 4♡, which they cannot make because of your heart holding or that partner will save over 4♡ with their heart shortage, which will turn out to be a phantom, or that you will play in 2♠ with 4♡ on your way. It does not take a great deal of imagination to give partner a hand such as:

♠ x
♡ AJxx
♢ Kxxx
♣ AKxx

which will pass 2♠ in its sleep to see what a daft opening it is. With the diamond finesse wrong you will probably not make 2♠, whereas a heart partial is cold and 4♡, whilst thin, is not a ridiculous contract. This takes us back to the old chestnut of should you pre-empt with an outside four card major? Twenty years ago everybody would have crossed you off their Christmas card list for a crime as hideous as that but times have changed. These days no-one bothers about having a four card major for a weak two or three opening but you need to show some sense about it. Change the hand above to:

♠ KQxxxx
♡ xxxx
♢ xx
♣ x

and I wouldn't think twice about opening 2♠ (or 3♠ at the right vulnerability and position). Now we have a good spade suit and bad hearts. Notice the difference this makes if we put it next to our hypothetical hand opposite of:

♠ x
♡ AJxx
♢ Kxxx
♣ AKxx

Now 4♡ has no play at all and even a heart partial is tricky. 2♠, however, would be rather unlucky to go down. You have avoided the foolish result of playing a partial going off with game makeable in the other major.

So finally what does a minimum and a maximum non-vulnerable weak two bid look like? This is obvious a matter for partnership discussion and there is no substitute for sitting down and making a joint decision on this matter. I would only emphasise again that you want to be looking at playability and offence to defence ratio rather than point count.

My own views are that, in a sound style:

♠ QJ109xx
♡ xx
◇ xxx
♣ xx

is an ideal minimum weak 2♠ and:

♠ J10xxxx
♡ x
◇ QJx
♣ Qxx

is an acceptable if flawed minimum weak two. At the other end of the scale I would regard:

♠ AQJxxx
♡ xx
◇ xxx
♣ xx

as an ideal maximum weak 2♠ (though many would open this 3♠) and:

♠ Kxxxxx
♡ xxx
◇ KQx
♣ x

as an acceptable maximum weak 2♠. However, I regard both:

♠ AKJ10xx
♡ x
◇ xxxx
♣ xx

and:

♠ KJ109xx
♡ x
♦ KQ10x
♣ xx

as much too strong non-vulnerable. It seems to me that you are very likely
to miss game if you open either of these hands 2♠. When considering a
move partner has to take into account that you may hold just QJ10xxx. I
regard the first of these hands as a routine 3♠, a good six card suit and no
outside values. The second hand I would open 1♠, as I am sure would
most experts today. 3♠ is misguided as you have so much playing
strength and such a good side suit. I suppose you could pass, but bridge is
a bidder's game and passing hands like these is losing tactics.

Again many players would regard my suggestions here as ridiculously
conservative and would regard 2♠ on:

♠ J10xxxx
♡ Qxx
♦ xxx
♣ x

as normal even in a fairly sound style. It is for partnerships to decide what
the acceptable limits are.

What about five card suits? If three level bids are regularly opened on
decent six card suits are weak twos opened on decent five card suits? The
answer to this question for most pairs is a definite yes.

Thus a hand such as:

♠ KQJ10x
♡ xxx
♦ xx
♣ xxx

is ideal for a five card 2♠ opening and:

♠ KJxxx
♡ xx
♦ Kxxx
♣ xx

is acceptable if that is your style. As always you need to exercise some
commonsense in this. I regard a weak 2♡ opening that I saw recently on:

♠ Axx
♡ Jxxxx
◊ Axxx
♣ x

('It says 5-9 points and a five card suit on our card, partner') as one of the silliest calls I have seen in a long time, for reasons that I hope are all too obvious.

Before you gaily adopt this idea, it is worth remembering that it puts considerable extra strain on the responder to have to deal with a weak two that may be either a five card or a six card suit. There is an enormous difference in playing strength between a minimum weak two with a five card suit and a maximum weak two with a six card suit. At the three level this difference in playing strength is not so important since the decision as to whether to bid on or not is sometimes a matter of luck and guesswork. Whether it is correct to bid frequently depends on how well the two hands mesh together. This cannot be determined when the auction starts at the three level; you just have to take a view and hope it is correct. This is not the case at the two level where you often have enough room to explore. Partner's first decision then is whether to move over the weak two at all. If you play a fairly tightly controlled set of criteria for weak twos then that decision is relatively easy. But of course this reduces the occasions on which you can open a weak two. On the other hand if the weak two can be anything from a minimum hand with a five card suit such as:

♠ KQxxx
♡ xxx
◊ xx
♣ xxx

to a maximum with a six card suit such as:

♠ K1098xx
♡ xx
◊ KQx
♣ xx

then the decision as to whether or not to respond is much more difficult.

Even knowing how good a fit the partnership has is complicated. 'Honour one', for example, is fine in support if partner has a six card suit but is a little thin if partner can have only a five card suit. Take a perfectly ordinary balanced hand opposite such as:

♠ Ax
♡ AQxx
◇ Axxx
♣ Jxx

opposite the hand with the six card suit 4♠ is extremely playable. OK, you need the trump break but if you avoid a heart lead you can try for diamonds 3-3 before having to fall back on the heart finesse. Definitely a game I would want to be in.

On the other hand opposite the five card suit even 3♠ has no play at all. Indeed you cannot guarantee 2♠. So to move on this hand risks a certain negative score opposite the first hand and not to move risks missing game on the second hand. The fact that the second hand has more points is pretty much irrelevant. You can add the ◇K to the first hand if you want to and 3♠ would still be a very poor contract, yet now you have a maximum weak two with a five card suit (and so might even get to game!). The point is that hands with six card suits are simply a lot more powerful that hands with five card suits. They simultaneously provide you with another winner in terms of the long trump; allow you to draw trumps more easily; allow you to ruff outside suits more easily; and have one less loser in them (the stray card that has now become a trump). This reasoning holds of course all the way up. Hands with seven card suits are more powerful than hands with six card suits, hands with eight card suits ... until we get to hands with thirteen card suits which most of us would agree are pretty powerful. Before you gaily allow weak twos on five card suits, then you should be aware of the problems this can cause the responding hand. Remember also that, if you believe the views of the school of good weak twos/bad weak threes in America, then a weak two is not the world's greatest strike weapon. Perhaps it is not worth it.

Another possible solution to whether or not you should open five card weak twos is gaining popularity amongst the cognoscenti in Britain at the moment. That is to play both six card and five card weak twos but to use separate bids for them. A common scheme is to use 2♡ and 2♠ as natural weak twos promising six card suits and to use 2◇ as showing a five card weak 2♡ or 2♠. This has the merit of solving the responding headache for partner. It does of course use up an entire bid just to distinguish between five and six card suits and it does have all the problems of artificial pre-empts associated with it (see later). However, if you fancy the idea give it a go.

Before we move on it is useful also for your partnership to make some decision about what to do about highly distributional hands. Hands which are 5-5 or 6-5 in particular. For example let us take:

♠ K10xxxx
♡ x
◇ x
♣ Axxxx

Opinions on what to do on hands like this vary across the expert community and across the world. Many players take the view that no opening bid describes them and so pass, hoping to be able to describe the hand better later on. That would have been the prevailing view fifteen years ago but naturally that is not the case now. Many modern players seem to regard it as a personal affront if they cannot bid at least once on every hand. A lot of players would now choose to open a hand such as the above 3♠ and players who subscribe to a wild pre-empting style might well try 4♠ non-vulnerable. If this turns out to be the wrong thing to do and clubs are a much better trump suit, or if partner misjudges the hand, relying on club defensive values, then they just shrug their shoulders. That is the risk you take. They argue that you are just as likely to get a good result since the opposition will be unaware of your long side suit, and hence your extra playing strength, as you are a bad result.

Certainly in Britain you would find nobody prepared to open this hand 2♠. They would argue that the hand has much too much playing strength for 2♠ and that partner will never be able to judge the auction. There is no doubt this is true, so if you do open it 2♠ you have to do something about showing your extra playing strength. Whilst unknown in Britain, this kind of weak two seems to be popular amongst experts from a number of countries, and in particular it appears in Austria. The Austrians seem quite happy to open 2♠ on such hands but are then absolutely fearless about showing the extra playability and length. The hand quoted above comes from a previous world championship and the auction proceeded:

2♠   Dble   Pass   3♡
4♣!

So, having opened his weak two, the player was then prepared to show the second suit at the four level opposite a passed partner.

It is entirely a matter of partnership understanding what is to be done on highly distributional hands of less than opening strength. There is no right answer to the problem. If there was a right answer then all the bridge world would be playing it by now and there would not be a problem. You merely have to go with what you find comfortable for you and your partner and what you find works for you.

So much for non-vulnerable weak twos in a sound style. What about vulnerable weak twos, again in a sound style? Well, the obvious answer is that they should be better. How much better? Depends on how worried you get about the prospect of going for -800 or -1100 on a really bad day. As always, we are not very concerned about points. Tricks are what matters, and even more so vulnerable. So in particular we should be concerned about suit quality for a vulnerable weak two. Apart from the obvious fact that the better your suit is (and particularly the better the intermediates are) the more tricks you will make with it, it is also a lot more difficult for the opposition to defend at the two level doubled if they have poor intermediates. A defender with AJ109 over you would be delighted to defend the hand doubled and the same hand under you would be quite content. Three trump tricks over you are almost guaranteed over the bid and very likely under the bid. Contrast that with a trump holding of AJ32 which would be nervous defending over the bid and suicidal defending under the bid. Here two trump tricks are the absolute maximum and that is not guaranteed. So intermediates are important not just to give you more tricks but to dissuade the opposition from defending the hand doubled even when that is right for them.

With the above in mind I personally do not mind much a weak two at game all on:

♠ QJ109xx
♡ xx
◇ xxx
♣ xx

though I would not do it at Red, nor without the ♠10, nor second in hand. If this gets doubled and goes for -1100, then I will have to apologise. However, in a sense that is not the worst aspect of 2♠ on this hand (though you may think it is pretty hard to get worse than -1100). The problem is that, expecting a better hand, partner will move forward and incur a minus score.

However:

♠ KQ10xxx
♡ xx
◇ xxx
♣ xx

in my opinion, is an entirely acceptable minimum vulnerable weak two.
Again this could go horribly wrong and you could concede a four figure
penalty. However, if you are worried about getting knocked over you
would never cross the road. The danger has to be weighed against the gain.
Passing decent six card suits cannot be right. A maximum weak two
vulnerable will be a hand with a good six card suit and could well look like
a hand that would open at the three level non-vulnerable. So I consider
both:

♠ AKJ10xx
♡ x
◇ xxxx
♣ xx

and:

♠ KJ10xxx
♡ x
◇ KJxx
♣ xx

as sensible maximum vulnerable weak 2♠ bids and I would also open:

♠ K10xxxx
♡ xx
◇ KQx
♣ xx

a vulnerable weak two and treat it as a maximum if I had a set of responses
that could distinguish between suit quality and point count (see later).
Here the suit is not up to much but passing this hand will be a losing tactic
in the long run and at least you have a compensating diamond trick(s) to
reduce the penalty if they get hold of you.

What about seven card suits? Particularly vulnerable there are hands with
seven card suits that simply will not be opened at the three level in a sound
pre-empting style.

Take for example:

♠ Qxxxxxx
♥ Kx
♦ xx
♣ xx

or:

♠ K10xxxxx
♥ QJx
♦ xx
♣ x

or even:

♠ 109xxxxx
♥ x
♦ Axx
♣ xx

These are not even close to a vulnerable 3♠ in a sound style. Should you therefore open them at the two level? As usual, opinion is divided on this issue. One view (which is the view I share) is that it is daft to pass seven card suits if there is a moderately sensible alternative and that therefore vulnerable weak twos with seven card suits not good enough for the three level is just sensible bridge. The opposite view is that no hand with a seven card suit should be opened a weak two bid. The argument here is exactly the same as that for opening both five and six card suits a weak two. Here, if you open both six and seven card suits a weak two, then partner will never be able to judge the hand because a hand with a seven card suit is just so much more powerful than a hand with a six card suit. If we compare a hand such as:

♠ KQxxxx
♥ xx
♦ xxx
♣ xx

with:

♠ K10xxxxx
♥ QJx
♦ xx
♣ x

you will see the difference in trick taking potential. These players would therefore be content to pass hands with seven card suits not suitable for the three level in order to allow the responder to weak twos greater knowledge of the specific hand type. This is certainly a sensible argument, just as it was for whether you should open five card weak twos.

It is silly to open both five and seven card suits weak twos at the same vulnerability. This really is a nightmare for partner. If they have to judge whether to try for game opposite a vulnerable weak two (and remember any vulnerable game that is 35% or better is a paying proposition) that can be anything from:

♠ KQJ10x
♥ xxx
♦ xx
♣ xxx

to:

♠ K10xxxxx
♥ QJx
♦ xx
♣ x

then partner might as well just start throwing dice without looking at their hand to decide whether to move or not.

So a sound style of weak twos is that on the whole they show six card suits; non-vulnerable this can include decent five card suits and vulnerable this can include seven card suits. You will have to decide whether you want to include five and/or seven card suits, bearing in mind the extra problems caused to the responding hand. What matters is that both members of the partnership are agreed on the values required for a weak two.

By the way, even if you do decide to include seven card suits in your vulnerable weak twos this does not make the problem of sub-minimum hands with long suits go away entirely. Consider this nightmare from last years Crockfords Final. At Red, second in hand you pick up:

♠ J9765432
♥ J
♦ J
♣ J105

and RHO passes. Any offers? Second in hand at Red is the position where your pre-empts are expected to be at their most sound. Surely partner has a right to expect significantly better than a jack high suit, so 3♠ hardly looks attractive. 2♠ is even sillier, however; partner will never play you for two extra cards in your suit. How is poor partner supposed to know that 40% of the time you will make six trump tricks opposite a singleton? For this reason half of the players who held the hand in the Crockfords Final chose to pass since there was simply no even vaguely sensible opening bid; the rest chose 3♠. You might be interested to know how they fared. Partner's hand was the obvious:

♠ —
♡ AQ98xx
◊ Ax
♣ AK9xx

Of those who opened 3♠ two were raised to 4♠, an action I entirely agree with. How can you expect a three loser trump suit for a Red three level pre-empt? This went off when the club finesse was wrong and nothing good happened in hearts. The other two guessed to bid 4♡, an action I do not agree with. This made when they could take a diamond ruff and just lose two trumps and a club. So it shows what I know! However, if you give partner a more sensible Red pre-empt such as:

♠ KQJ10xxx
♡ x
◊ xxx
♣ xx

you will see how sensible the raise to 4♠ is. Here 4♠ is cold whereas 4♡ is a very poor contract. Of those who passed second in hand the decision fell on them much later after partner had shown a huge hand with six hearts and five clubs. The winning decision was to bid 4♡; as the cards lay 5♣ could not be made.

Weak Two Bids in a Wild Style

If you decide on a wild pre-emptive style then what should you be opening weak twos on? Obviously the first criterion is that it should be weaker than what you are prepared to open three level pre-empts on. So the starting point is your bottom line for a three level bid, both vulnerable and non-vulnerable. If we deal with non-vulnerable offerings first, then what is your bottom line? Is king to six your minimum suit? Or jack to six? Or six small? Or queen to five? Once this is decided then you will know what a typical non-vulnerable weak two will look like. One of the first things that is clear is that for wild pre-emptors weak twos non-vulnerable on six card suits are virtually unheard of. Almost without exception six card suits non-vulnerable are opened at the three level. I suppose something like:

♠ xx
♡ 10xxxxx
◇ xxx
♣ xx

would open 2♡ rather than 3♡ but a really wild pre-emptor might not baulk at 3♡ even on this. So in a wild pre-emptive style weak twos non-vulnerable pretty must promise no better than a five card suit. Moreover most wild pre-emptors have no qualms about suit quality. So 2♠ on:

♠ KQxxx
♡ xxx
◇ xxx
♣ xx

or:

♠ Qxxxx
♡ x
◇ Kxxx
♣ xxx

or even:

♠ 98743
♡ xx
◇ xx
♣ QJxx

(yes, I did see this one at the table) would be considered normal for wild pre-emptors.

Does it get any worse? Well, depending on your philosophy and bottle, yes, it does. It can get a lot worse if you want it to.

On one of the few occasions Brian Senior was opposite me (it didn't happen very often; Brian rapidly got tired of my ability to let cold off games through the gate. Odd really.) He opened a weak two on:

♠ xxx
♡ xxxx
◇ Jxx
♣ xxx

first in hand at love all! You may well be wondering what suit he chose. In fact it was diamonds. Brian claimed later that he was showing where his values where, though the plural seems redundant in this case. Brian has a penchant for particularly offbeat weak 2◇ openings. Previous fine offerings have included:

♠ Qxxx
♡ x
◇ Kxxx
♣ xxxx

and:

♠ xxx
♡ x
◇ Qxxx
♣ Qxxxx

Brian maintains that a very random 2◇ opening is as effective as a wild 2♡ or 2♠ and nowhere near as dangerous since partner needs so much more to even try for game that you rarely get overboard when partner has a good hand and partner rarely takes a very expensive save since the five level is much more dangerous than the four level. There would appear to be some merit in these arguments. Certainly most people I know who play a weak 2◇ allow a very loose style for the 2◇ opening with just about any five card suit acceptable. Presumably this works for them or they wouldn't keep doing it. It does of course need to be clearly on the convention card.

In a similar vein Roman Smolski is known for his less than sound pre-empts. He once opened a multi 2◇ on:

♠ xxx
♡ xxx
◇ xxx
♣ Qxxx

Perhaps fortunately he was not called upon to bid again. At the end of the hand partner asked him, which major he was going to show a weak two in and Roman replied that he hadn't quite decided yet.

By the way, Roman is now one of the few players around who plays natural weak two bids in all four suits. No, he doesn't play a strong club. What does he do with Acol 2♣ openers? Opens them at the one level and sees if somebody bids! These days someone almost always does.

So you can see the kind of lengths that wild pre-emptors will go to to get in the auction. Now I am not saying this is right or sound or that in the long run these methods will not be tried and found wanting. It may be that they will be consigned to the bridge garbage heap along with the micro no-trump and strong pass after the opponent's opening bid. All I am saying is that a number of wild pre-emptors will make these kind of bids non-vulnerable (and particularly at Green) and all wild pre-emptors will open pretty much any kind of five card suit at the two level. If that is the style of pre-empt you wish to play and you believe that is winning bridge, then go ahead and try it out. It does put considerable strain on the responding hand though. About an 18 count and honour to three support is minimum for even thinking about making a game try opposite a wild major suit weak two and rather more opposite 2♢.

How about wild vulnerable weak twos? Even wild pre-emptors generally have some respect for the vulnerability. This is not universal though. Remember the Meckstroth-Rodwell hand in Chapter 1, 10 to six diamonds and an outside Qx for a Red 3♢? Again your limits, both upper and lower for a vulnerable weak two in a wild style, will depend on your lower limit for a vulnerable three bid. If your lower limit for a vulnerable three bid is KQJ to six then a vulnerable weak two would be less than this, say KQ to six. If on the other hand you are prepared to open:

♠ QJxxxx
♡ –
♢ QJxx
♣ xxx

3♠ vulnerable and damn the torpedoes, then your vulnerable weak two will be less than that. Most wild pre-emptors of my acquaintance would regard QJ to six as a rock bottom minimum for a weak two vulnerable.

5
RESPONDING TO NATURAL WEAK TWOS

Responding to weak twos is generally a lot easier than responding to weak threes. This is for exactly the same reason that defending against weak twos is so much easier than defending against weak threes. You have more room. You have the remainder of the two level and all of the three level available before you have to commit yourself to game or not. In particular you have 2NT available. Everybody (and I mean everybody) plays 2NT as a conventional call after partner has opened a weak two. There seems very little merit in having 2NT as a natural game try since it will almost never be right to play in exactly 2NT, so partner will almost always bid. Indeed if you read Kokish he will tell that you should always treat 2NT as forcing every time partner has shown a six card suit (and pretty much on every other occasion as well actually). Thus 2NT is a conventional bid asking partner to describe the nature of their weak two bid. There are, as always, various schemes on the market. These fall broadly into three categories and I will describe each of them.

Until relatively recently the most common responses played were the so-called Blue Team responses, called this not surprisingly as they were the responses played by the all conquering Italian Blue Team to their weak two bids. These are a codified set of responses whereby after 2NT opener rebids as follows:

3♣   Shows a minimum point count and minimum suit quality.
3♦   Shows a minimum point count and good suit quality.
3♥   Shows a maximum point count but minimum suit quality.
3♠   Shows a maximum point count and good suit quality.
3NT   Shows a one loser suit at worst.

(In the original responses 3NT showed a solid suit – at least AKQ to six. That's how constructive the Blue Team weak twos were! I do not know anyone who opens solid suits a weak two now. They are opened one or three (or even four). It is thus silly to have a bid for something that never comes up. 3NT can thus be played to show a suit that will play for one loser opposite a singleton – a minimum of KQJxxx or AQJxxx and preferably the 10 as well.)

Of course, what is a minimum or maximum point count and what is a good suit quality is very much a function of what kind of style of weak two you are playing. In a sound style, after a non-vulnerable 2♠ opening a hand such as:

♠ Q10xxxx
♡ Qxx
◇ Qxx
♣ x

would of course respond 3♣ to the 2NT enquiry whereas:

♠ K10xxxx
♡ x
◇ KQx
♣ xxx

would respond 3♡ and:

♠ KQ109xx
♡ xxx
◇ xx
♣ xx

would respond 3◇ (good suit but not good enough for 3NT).

Playing a wild style the first hand would respond 3◇ (this is a good suit, you have six of them after all!) and the other two would probably open at the three level.

In a wild style:

♠ KQxxx
♡ xxx
◇ KJx
♣ xx

would be a 3♠ bid (good suit for a wild weak two and maximum point count) whereas a 3♣ bid would be whatever pile of garbage is your bottom limit.

Perhaps:

♠ Jxxxx
♡ xx
◇ xxxx
♣ xx

or something of that order. I'm sure you get the idea anyway.

The Blue Team responses are essentially designed to bid games if you have enough points and a good enough trump suit. They are thus well suited to balanced hands opposite the weak two. What the Blue Team responses do not do is give an indication where the outside values (if any) lie. It is thus impossible to tell if the mesh of cards between the two hands is good or bad. Blue Team responses are not very suitable for making game tries with distributional hands or for bidding minimum point count but well fitting hands to game. For these reasons the Blue Team responses are falling rather out of favour these days and are being replaced by one of two other styles of responses. In the first style the weak two opener always rebids their own suit with a minimum, bids an outside high card with a maximum or 3NT with a good (one loser) suit. So in this style, after a 2♠ opening bid and a 2NT enquiry:

3♣/◇/♡   Would show a maximum with a high card in ♣/◇/♡.
3♠   Would show a minimum.
3NT   Would show a one loser suit.

Thus on the example hands above, assuming a sound style and non-vulnerable:

♠ Q10xxxx
♡ Qxx
◇ Qxx
♣ x

would respond 3♠ to the 2NT enquiry whereas:

♠ K10xxxx
♡ x
◇ KQx
♣ xxx

would respond 3◇ and:

♠ KQ109xx
♡ xxx
◇ xx
♣ xx

would respond 3♠ (not good enough for 3NT and otherwise minimum).

In a wild style the first hand would respond 3◇ whereas of the other two hands suggested for a wild 2♠ opening:

♠ KQxxx
♡ xxx
◇ KJx
♣ xx

would respond 3◇ and:

♠ Jxxxx
♡ xx
◇ xxxx
♣ xx

would naturally enough respond 3♠.

The advantage of this method over the Blue Team responses is that some idea of the degree of fit is found as well as the information as to whether partner is maximum or minimum. I will show you one quick example from actual play as to how this can help. Partner opens 2♠ at Red playing a very sound style and you are looking at:

♠ K10x
♡ Axxxx
◇ Kx
♣ Qxx

At any other vulnerability and style this is a clear pass (though you might raise to 3♠ pre-emptively!) but the player felt he had enough for 2NT. Partner responded 3◇ which suited his hand rather well since the ◇K and the doubleton daimond were both likely to be useful so he leapt to 4♠. Partner obliged with the highly suitable:

♠ AQxxxx
♡ x
◇ Q10xx
♣ xx

and ten tricks came home for +620. Notice the advantage of these responses in this case over the Blue Team responses The degree of fit in the side suit is discovered. Playing Blue Team responses this hand would have responded 3♠ and there would have been no way of telling if the 2♠ opener had the above hand or:

$$\begin{array}{l} \spadesuit \text{ AQxxxx} \\ \heartsuit \text{ xx} \\ \diamondsuit \text{ x} \\ \clubsuit \text{ Kxxx} \end{array}$$

which would have made 4♠ very poor.

The third possible set of responses are rarely seen in Britain but I will include them for completeness. In this style over 2NT the opener shows any singleton they have regardless of the strength of the hand and rebids their suit with no singleton and a minimum or 3NT with no singleton and a maximum. So, after 2♠–Pass–2NT, for example:

3♣/◇/♡   Show a singleton ♣/◇/♡.
3♠   Shows a minimum with no singleton.
3NT   Shows a maximum with no singleton.

These responses are only really sensible if your weak twos are based on six cards suits when singletons are reasonably likely. If your weak twos are frequently on five card suits then these responses have little merit since you do not have singletons nearly enough of the time. Most of the time you are simply bidding three of your suit or 3NT. These responses, as I am sure is obvious, are very helpful if you are enquiring with a weak suit outside such as three small or jack to four. Then, if partner shows shortage in that suit, you are often able to bid a very low point count game. The problem with the responses, as I am sure is equally obvious, is that unless the response hits a weak suit in responder's hand it is not so much use to you. In particular it does not tell you if partner is maximum or minimum or anything about suit quality. Hence it is often difficult to judge whether or not you have a reasonable play for game if the singleton does not hit such a perfect mesh with your hand.

Well, you pays your money and takes your choice. My personal preference is for the second method whereby high card features are shown but if anything else attracts you then go ahead and try it. You may find it works for you. Before we leave the 2NT response many pairs play that the three level responses are the only responses the weak two opener is allowed to make. However, some pairs allow the opener to respond at the four level on suitable hands. There are two possibilities for this. The first, and universally played method in Britain, is that a four level response shows a good maximum with a singleton in the suit bid. So after:

2♠	Pass	2NT	Pass

♠ AJ10xxx
♡ xxx
◇ x
♣ Kxx

might choose to bid 4◇. The other possibility is that the bids are natural, showing the kind of extreme two suiters mentioned earlier on. So after the same auction as above:

♠ Axxxxx
♡ x
◇ x
♣ Kxxxx

would respond 4♣. This method only makes any sense of course if such hands are acceptable weak twos in your style. Either method and particularly the first is very dangerous. The problem is that you have gone past 3NT which could well be where partner wants to play opposite your shortage. You may have left partner with no winning option. The positive aspect of them is that they can make slam bidding a lot easier if that is in partner's mind as you can immediately show your maximum and shortage. A compromise is to reserve the four level responses to show a void and a good suit. This way they come up less often and it is less likely that 3NT is the correct contract opposite a void.

So much for the 2NT enquiry to weak two bids; what about all the other possible responses to weak twos? Firstly it makes obvious sense that all direct raises should be pre-emptive just as they are after weak threes. Since you have the 2NT enquiry to find out about partner's hand there is absolutely no need for any raise to be a game try. It is far more sensible to continue to apply the pressure by using all direct raises as pre-emptive. So sequences such as:

2♠	Pass	3♠

or:

2◇	Pass	4◇

are all pre-emptive. Similarly raises to game may be highly pre-emptive in nature but may also be any hand that believes it has a decent play for game opposite partner's bid. So raise 2♠ to 4♠ on any of the following hands non-vulnerable:

> ♠ Axxx
> ♡ x
> ◊ xxxx
> ♣ xxxx

or:

> ♠ Kxxx
> ♡ AKxx
> ◊ Axxx
> ♣ x

or:

> ♠ Kxx
> ♡ xxx
> ◊ x
> ♣ AKxxxx

or:

> ♠ xxx
> ♡ AKQx
> ◊ KQxx
> ♣ AQ

On the first hand they will doubtless double you, but what do you care? They have a certain game on and a possible slam that you have made it very difficult to find. 4♠ doubled is probably going for only about -500 which is fine. On the second hand you expect to make 4♠ opposite any sensible weak two, so go ahead and bid it. Do not mess around with a 2NT enquiry that can serve no purpose since you intend to bid game anyway. On the third hand you might make 4♠ and you might not depending on partner's hand and the degree of fit. On the other hand it is quite likely that the opposition can make something and possibly even game. Curiously, if you can make game, the more likely it is that they can make game as well, since both sides will have a double fit. Do not give them the chance to get together and discover their combined assets. Bid 4♠ and give them the last guess not you. 4♠ is another example of a two-way shot; you win every time one side or the other can make game. On the fourth hand you clearly cannot make a slam despite your high point count. Partner will need a one loser trump suit and the ◊ A, too much for a weak two. So the only question is which game? 3NT superficially has some appeal but there is too much danger of your being locked out of the spade suit. If partner's suit is QJ10 to six for example you will look very silly unless the spades are 2-2 (and even then a club lead might defeat 3NT), whereas 4♠ will always be a sensible contract. It is hard to see how this can be worse than the club finesse and may be simply cold. Curiously, it would be worth trying for 3NT if your spades were better.

Change the hand to:

> ♠ Kxx
> ♡ AQxx
> ◊ KQxx
> ♣ AQ

and now it might be worth enquiring with 2NT. If partner bids 3NT showing a one loser suit you can pass this knowing that you are in a 100% contract.

On the whole, however, you should bid game in the major immediately whenever you think it is a sensible shot. Apart from anything else the more types of hand patterns that you can bid game on in tempo the more problems you will give the opponents. Sometimes they will not double you when you have been pre-emptive and sometimes they will double when you were bidding the hand to make. If you are always pre-emptive for a leap to game and you route all good hands through 2NT just to lengthen the auctions, you will be a very easy opponent to play against.

This leaves us finally with changes of suit. Simple chances of suit at either the two or level such as:

	2♡	Pass	2♠

or:

	2♡	Pass	3◊

or:

	2◊	Pass	2♡

are almost always played as natural. They can be played as either forcing, invitational, non-forcing or fit-showing. That seems to about cover all the bases. My own preference is to play these bids as invitational but not forcing, particularly in the majors. It seems to me that you have to be able to make a game try in a major opposite a weak two on a six card suit and a reasonable hand. Without this it is very difficult to see how you can go about bidding to four of a major sensibly. So, playing a sound style, I would bid 2♠ over 2♡ on:

> ♠ AQxxxx
> ♡ x
> ◇ Kx
> ♣ KQJx

Similarly I would also bid 2♠ over 2◇ on this hand. This may seem slightly perverse since we have already found a perfectly good diamond fit but if you think about this it is sensible. There is no game apart from 4♠ that has any chance; 3NT will lack the stops and/or the tricks and 5◇ is just miles away. So if game is to be made, 4♠ it will have to be and that means you must introduce your very decent six card major. Minor suits are for wimps, I believe someone once said. Give partner a perfectly sensible:

> ♠ Kx
> ♡ xxx
> ◇ QJ10xxx
> ♣ xx

and you will see the logic of this approach. 4♠ is extremely playable here without getting close to any other game. OK, I have given you perfectly fitting cards but the hand is a minimum in a sound style; I could have given partner a better hand. Whether or not you will bid game of course is another matter! I would certainly pass 2♠ on the above hand, happy that we have arrived in a very playable spot.

By the way the above hand is not worth more than 2♠ even over a sound weak two since no guarantee of a fit is present. If you take a stronger action partner is bound to turn up with:

> ♠ x
> ♡ KJx
> ◇ Q10xxxx
> ♣ xxx

or even:

♠ −
♡ KJx
◊ A109xxx
♣ xxxx

when you will end up in a variety of silly contracts. In a similar vein I would bid 3♡ over 2♠ on the same hand with the majors reversed. Obviously this sequence is more cramped than the others but nevertheless you can see plenty of hands where game will be playable in hearts, so you should try for it. Incidentally I would bid 2♠ on the above hand even over a wild pre-empt, in this case not so much because I think game may be on but because 2♠ may well be a better contract. It is certainly likely to be better than 2♡ and may be better than 2◊. After all king one is not great support for a wild pre-empt, particularly if it might look like one of Brian Senior's efforts.

Over these game tries the weak two opener can pass, bid game, raise if that is possible or make a game try if that is available. If you think about this, all new suits from the opener should be game tries with support for responder's suit. So after:

2♡   Pass   2♠   Pass

with:

♠ Kxx
♡ AJxxxx
◊ xx
♣ xx

bid 4♠. Partner can hardly expect any more. Honour to three spades and the ♡A must surely give a play for game opposite any sensible try.

With:

♠ Kx
♡ QJxxxx
◊ Kxx
♣ xx

bid 3◊. You do not have enough to insist on game now but you are worth a try. 3◊ will show where your outside values are, which should enable partner to assess the degree of fit and bid accordingly. Notice how much more useful this bid will be to partner than simply raising 2♠ to 3♠.

Finally, with:

♠ Kxx
♡ AJxxxx
◇ xxx
♣ x

bid 4♣. You have a great hand in support of spades so you can bid 4♣, which logically should be a splinter. This probably will not have much effect but just occasionally partner will have the right hand to bid a slam over this effort from you. Give partner:

♠ AQxxxx
♡ x
◇ KQJ
♣ Axx

and slam is excellent, yet partner could not possibly move if you just made the lazy bid of 4♠.

If the response to the weak two is three of a minor, then I prefer to play this as primarily showing a good suit with an eye to 3NT. Opener is expected to pass with no fit, show any NT stopper with some degree of fit, or in exceptional circumstances bid 3NT themselves. So I would respond 3◇ to 2♡ on:

♠ xx
♡ xx
◇ AKJxxxx
♣ Ax

If partner passes fine and if partner bids 3♠ showing a spade stopper we can confidently bid 3NT with the expectation of good play for the contract. Thus:

♠ xxx
♡ KQ10xxx
◇ xx
♣ xx

would pass 3◇.

♠ Kxx
♡ QJxxxx
◇ Qx
♣ xx

would bid 3♠ and we would bid 3NT. It is true that this is no contract on a club lead and anyway needs the spade finesse but minimum point count games of this kind, particularly when you have eight running tricks, are overall a paying proposition.

Finally:

♠ Kx
♡ Q109xxx
◊ xxx
♣ Kx

can take a pot at 3NT. The hand has a stop in both the other suits and, whilst there is no fitting honour for partner, three small should hopefully be sufficient to make it a one loser suit. You may well be able to scramble nine tricks, particularly after a blind lead.

If all suits are constructive but non-forcing, what do we do when we have a genuine force to game with a suit of our own? To resurrect an example from Chapter 2 what do we do if partner opens 2♠ and we have:

♠ A
♡ AKQJxxxx
◊ xx
♣ AK?

We are at least in better shape than when partner opened 3♠ when we had little choice but to pot 4♡. Here we have an extra level of room and can make use of it. The solution is to bid our forcing enquiry of 2NT. Whatever partner's response we then plan to introduce our heart suit. Since we could have made an invitational 3♡ bid immediately this must logically be forcing. Assuming you are playing my preferred responses, partner will probably rebid 3♠ (do you expect them to have better than a minimum when you have all this lot?) and now you will be endplayed into 4♡. But you are no worse off than you were before.

You may, however, get some more useful information. If partner bids 3◊, for example, slam is now very likely. You can continue with 3♡ (natural and forcing) and whatever partner bids you can continue the auction to try and screw a diamond cuebid out of them. Even if partner bids 3♣ hope is not over; there is still room for partner to have a diamond singleton and you should be able to sort this out.

Take for example this pair of hands:

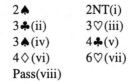

♠ KQxxxx		♠ A
♡ xx		♡ AKQJxxxx
◊ x		◊ xx
♣ Qxxx		♣ AK

The auction might proceed:

2♠	2NT(i)
3♣(ii)	3♡(iii)
3♠(iv)	4♣(v)
4◊(vi)	6♡(vii)
Pass(viii)	

(i)   Enquiry.

(ii)   Clearly a decent 2♠ opener so show the club feature.

(iii) Natural and FG.

(iv) You could raise hearts here with a clear conscience but it hardly looks wrong to emphasise the decent spades.

(v)   Partner might not know what is going on here but should get a diamond cuebid out of them if they have one.

(vi) I've no idea what is going on but this looks the right thing to do.

(vii) Thank you.

(viii) Sounds like partner wants to play there to me.

Finally, what about jumps in new suits? As usual these can be played any way you like but common methods are splinters agreeing partner's suit; fit jumps showing a fit for partner and a decent suit of your own or suit setting and demanding a cuebid. Of these the first two are the most common and my preference is for splinters, though there are increasing numbers of adherents for fit jumps. So if playing splinters we would respond 4♣ to 2♡ on:

♠ Axx
♡ AQxx
◊ AQJxx
♣ x

Most of the time this will not get us very far but, if partner can cuebid 4◊ on a suitable hand (i.e. one without wasted ♣ values for a start), then we could well have a cold slam. For example the right six count (the red kings) from partner makes it cold. There is thus no excuse for laziness.

So much for my preferred methods. What about the other options? I do not intend to spend very long on these but will include a brief description. If any of them interest you then try them out. You will be able to find a fuller description in the bridge magazines. Forcing responses are very rarely played these days. Hands that want to force are relatively rare (particularly opposite modern pre-empts) and can be dealt with in other ways. Non-forcing responses make a lot more sense if you are playing wild pre-empts. Just as non-forcing responses can be seen to be sensible over wild three bids so non-forcing responses can be seen to be sensible over wild weak twos. The style is the same as for three bids. That is, responses such as:

$$2\heartsuit \qquad Pass \qquad 2\spadesuit$$

or:

$$2\spadesuit \qquad Pass \qquad 3\diamondsuit$$

are essentially non-forcing and may be purely corrective in nature but opener is entitled to move with a suitable hand. So after:

$$2\heartsuit \qquad Pass \qquad 2\spadesuit \qquad Pass$$

♠ Kxx
♡ QJxxx
◇ Qxxx
♣ x

would certainly bid since you have such an excellent hand for spades.

Finally, fit bids have the same advantages and disadvantages as they have over three level pre-empts. They work very well when they come up but do not allow you to bid in any way constructively without a fit. Playing fit responses an ideal bid of 3◇ over 2♡ would be something like:

♠ xx
♡ Kxx
◇ AQJxx
♣ xxx

Here we want to suggest that partner leads a diamond against the opponents' contract but do not wish to mislead them about what suit we wish to play in. 3◇ allows us to get our lead director in and still allows partner to know that we have heart support. Partner is also welcome to leap to 4♡ if so inclined in the light of this knowledge. For example, if partner holds:

♠ xxx
♡ Axxxxx
♢ Kxx
♣ x

4♡ is a very playable game. Quite what the opponents are doing remaining silent with two solid fits and half the pack between them I'm not sure about but stranger things have happened. All very nice when it works, I'm just not convinced that it is worth the loss of all natural bids for these occasional, albeit very visible gains.

Artificial Pre-empts

Roll up! Roll up! Get you choice of pre-empt here. The 1980s in particular saw an explosion of artificial destructive weapons from which partnerships could choose. A lot of these have made it into the '90s as well, some of them with a general licence, some restricted and some experimental. Amongst these are:

2♣ is Acol or a weak 2♢
Multi-coloured 2♢
One Legged Multi-coloured 2♢
Polish 2♢
Tartan Two bids
Rainbow Two bids
Muilderberg Two bids
2NT is a weak pre-empt anywhere
2NT is a minor suit pre-empt
2NT shows both minors
2NT shows a major and a minor
3♣ shows both minors
Transfer pre-empts including 3♣ = Red pre-empt,
                              3♢ = major pre-empt
3♣ or 3♢ or 3♠ is any solid suit
etc. etc. etc.

It is not the job of this book to look at artificial pre-empts. Indeed it would be twice the length if I were to attempt even a cursory description of all the various toys available for artificially disrupting the opponents' auction. There is no doubt that such bids can be very valuable for two main reasons. Firstly, they allow you to open more weak hands than before. If you play any of the weak two-suited gadgets then you can pre-empt more often and with more safety. Since pre-empts work (otherwise we would all have given up doing it long ago) this must be good news. Secondly, an artificial pre-empt forces the opposition to have some form of defence to it which increases the chances of confusion amongst their ranks. It is true that very many of these bids can be defended in the same kind of generic manner so a specific defence for every artificial pre-empt is unnecessary. Nevertheless there is still the potential for a mis-understanding. I mentioned earlier, however, that there is now a reaction against these artificial pre-empts and many players are returning to natural weak twos and threes. Why is this if artificial pre-empts are so good? The answer of course is there is no such thing as a free lunch and in the case of artificial pre-empts many players have decided that the cost outweighs the benefits.

There are two main problems associated with artificial pre-empts. The first is that most artificial pre-empts require the partner of the opener to respond. This automatically gives the opposition a second bite at the cherry. A very good example of the extra room given to the opposition by an artificial pre-empt is the multi-coloured 2◇. In its classical form the multi showed either a weak 2♡, a weak 2♠ or various strong hands. Let us assume that you have opened a multi coloured 2◇ and in this case you have a weak 2♠. You open 2◇ and your LHO can choose to bid or not. They do not have to since they know that they will get another chance since your partner must respond. Hence immediately the opposition can distinguish between two ranges of hand by bidding now or passing and then bidding. Let's say LHO passes and partner responds 2♡ (to play opposite a weak 2♡). Provided that they are reasonably sure that you do not have hearts (perhaps because they do) your RHO also has two choices: pass or bid. So again your RHO can distinguish between two ranges of hand. If RHO chooses to pass you will bid 2♠ and both opponents have another chance.

Hence the opponents get a minimum of two bids each (and it may be more in certain sequences) to describe their hands to each other. Contrast this with a natural weak 2♠ opening. Your LHO must make a decision as to whether to bid or not now since they might not get another chance. 2♠ could become the final contract. Hence somehow bids from LHO must be made to cover the entire range from a marginal call to a game-forcing rock-crusher and both balanced and unbalanced hands. The same is true of RHO if 2♠ is passed round to them. Passing and awaiting developments would leave them with a long wait, so this is their only chance to act. Bids here must cover everything from a minimum protection to the same game-forcing rock-crusher. The only information they have available is that partner felt unable to bid over 2♠. I hope you see the difference. The natural pre-empt forces a decision on each opponent immediately; the artificial pre-empt usually allows both opponents a couple of goes and hence makes it easier for them to sort out their hands.

The other difficulty with artificial pre-empts is that frequently opener's suit(s) are not known on the first round of the auction. This can cause the opponents grief if they do not what they are doing since they can become unsure which of their doubles are takeout and which penalties. However, it also means that you cannot increase the pre-empt unless you have support for all of partner's potential combinations. This often leaves you badly placed in the auction.

Let us look again at the multi as an example and use a hand in response from earlier in the chapter. Partner has opened a multi 2◇ and you hold:

♠ Axxx
♡ x
◇ xxxx
♣ xxxx

Whether or not your RHO bids you cannot afford to pre-empt on this hand. You will have to bid 2♡ (to play opposite hearts) since you obviously do not want any part of this if partner has hearts. That is fine if partner does have hearts but just occasionally partner has spades. In that case you would dearly loved to have bid 4♠ but it is too late now. By the time you discover (if ever) that partner has spades the opposition will have got together and determined their combined assets. If you believe that the opposition are going to sit there quietly and let you bid:

2◇	Pass	2♡	Pass
2♠	Pass	?	

so that you can now bid 4♠ pre-emptively then you must be used to playing against zombies. The opposition will bid and find their heart fit or no trumps and that will be that. Contrast this with a natural 2♠ opening from partner. Now you can bid 4♠ in your sleep and let the opponents sort that out as best they may. Your pre-empt has now become as effective as possible.

The classic example of the rise and fall of an artificial pre-empt is the multi. When it first appeared on the tournament scene it was devastating. Nobody knew how to defend against it; everybody was worried about bidding over it in case it was one of the strong hands; takeout doubles were misinterpreted as penalty doubles and vice versa. Pairs played in silly contracts – no less a pair than Belladonna-Garozzo played in 4♡ on a 2-2 fit after a multi 2♢ opening against them. In short, users of the multi got away with murder and just racked up the points. However, I do not know an expert pair in Britain who any longer play a classical multi (though it is still quite popular on the Continent of Europe). Now almost all pairs have a sensible and effective defence to it and can avoid the ludicrous results. Today the twin problems of giving the opponents more room and not being able to pre-empt efficiently outweigh the advantages of the multi and so it has died a death at the top level in this country.

I am not, let me hasten to add, suggesting that you should not play artificial pre-empts. Play all the toys you want if that is the way your mind and partnership runs. All I am saying is that you should be aware of the downside of such bids as well as the advantages.

6
PRE-EMPTS IN COMPETITION

So far I have concentrated on pre-emptive opening bids. In this chapter I want to look at just some of the pre-emptive tools available in the field of competitive bidding. In the old days when you had a good hand the opponents left you alone. When both you and your partner had good hands then the opponents kept a hallowed silence for you. Those days are long gone and they ain't never coming back. Now people open on tram tickets, overcall on bus tickets, raise on used postage stamps and jump raise on last week's losing lottery tickets. Well if the opponents are doing all that, why don't you have a go at inflicting some trouble with a few pre-emptive calls yourself? The ideas are not difficult. Essentially we define almost all direct raises as pre-emptive and find some other way of bidding genuine raises.

We Open the Bidding

Let's start with an easy one. For example, the auction goes:

1♠   Dble   ??

Almost all players believe that 3♠ should be pre-emptive here, typically showing a raise to two but promising four trumps. The argument is that, if the opposition want to get into the auction, we should make it as difficult as possible for them by getting the bidding as high as possible as fast as possible. What do you do with a good raise? Most players bid 2NT to show a good raise to at least 3♠. 2NT is unnecessary as a natural call now as we can redouble with that hand.

All very standard stuff. However, almost no pairs below the expert level appreciate that you can use exactly the same principle on the second round of the auction after the auction has gone something like:

1♦   Pass   1♠   Dble

Now we can play: 3♠ is pre-emptive.

2NT is a good raise to at least 3♠.

Redouble shows a hand that would normally rebid 2NT.

So we can bid 3♠ on:

♠ Axxx
♡ xx
◇ AQJxx
♣ xx

Surely it must be sensible to stop LHO bidding hearts at the three level which they could do in comfort if we had to just raise to 2♠. Here we may force a decision on LHO as to whether to pass quietly and not tell partner about the fit or overbid with 4♡. The more you can make the opponents guess, the more often they will guess wrong. On a good hand with support such as:

♠ AKxx
♡ xxx
◇ AKxxx
♣ x

we can bid 2NT to show a full value raise to at least 3♠.

Finally on hands that would have bid 2NT without the double such as:

♠ xx
♡ AQx
◇ KQJxx
♣ AQx

we can redouble. We can always bid 2NT on the next round if that is appropriate and this way we may end up defending a two level contract doubled if that is partner's wish.

The situation is no different if the opponents overcall rather than double. Almost without exception good partnerships now play that all raises of opener's suit after intervention are pre-emptive.

So after either:

| 1♡ | 1♠ | ? | or | 1♡ | 2◇ | ? |

to bid 2♡ on:

♠ xxx
♡ Kxx
◇ xx
♣ Qxxxx

would be considered normal. If you do not get your support in now you are likely to be frozen out of the auction altogether, unable to show your minimum but potentially useful values. It also takes away the cheap cuebid of 2♡ from the opposition. Provided that partner does not expect more (and certainly does not expect extra values in the old-fashioned idea of a free bid showing extras) then this is perfectly safe. In a similar vein, non-vulnerable (and particularly at Green), most partnerships would consider a jump raise to 3♡ as routine on:

♠ xx
♡ Kxxx
◇ xx
♣ Qxxxx

after either:

1♡   1♠   ?   or   1♡   2◇   ?

That is, the bid is pre-emptive and has no constructive overtones to it at all. You can imagine what kind of trouble this can cause the overcalling side. In the first case fourth hand may have had a comfortable raise to 2♠ if you had bid just 2♡. Now they have to decide whether to pass and leave partner in the dark about their support or stretch to bid 3♠. On the other hand they may have a good raise to 3♠, a hand on which they would have jumped to 3♠ if allowed to. You have denied them that opportunity. So now a 3♠ bid could conceal anything from a stretched 2♠ bid to a sound 3♠ bid not good enough for game. How is the overcaller supposed to know which? They cannot, which means your pre-empt has done its job.

Other problems for the opposition can also occur. For example, after:

1♡   1♠   2♡

fourth in hand would have felt comfortable bidding 3◇ on:

♠ xx
♡ xx
◇ AKJxxx
♣ xxx

and that could well have led to a making 3NT for the opposition. You have denied them that opportunity. Now they have little choice but to pass with gritted teeth. It is hardly sound to start winging this suit around at the four level.

In the second sequence when a minor suit has been overcalled, the pre-empt can still cause problems, even if fourth in hand is lucky enough to own some spades. Take for example this hand:

♠ KQxxxx
♡ xx
◇ Jx
♣ xxx

After:

1♡   2◇   2♡   ?

we can bid 2♠ in our sleep but are you so sanguine about it if you have to bid 3♠ over 3♡? Or how about:

♠ AJ9xx
♡ Axx
◇ Qxx
♣ xx

Here you have lively chances of game opposite a 2◇ overcall. After:

1♡   2◇   2♡

you can bid 2♠ if that is forcing in your methods (to be fair, I would bid spades even if it were non-forcing as spades seem the most likely game) and then try for no trumps if that yields no joy. But what about:

1♡   2◇   3♡   ?

You have to choose between 3♠ and 3NT and do it now. 3♠ may well end play partner into a raise on what turns out to be inadequate support. Bid 3♠ and partner is pretty much forced to raise on:

♠ Qx
♡ xx
◇ AKxxxx
♣ QJx

giving 4♠ no genuine play at all, with 3NT on a finesse through the opening bidder. Bid 3NT and partner will inevitably put down:

♠ Kxx
♡ x
◇ KJ10xxx
♣ Axx

giving 3NT no play at all with 4♠ and 5◇ eminently sensible.

There is no doubt about it, pre-emptive jump raises in competition cause the opponents a lot of headaches. If you have been finding that the opposition always seem to be up too high for your comfort after you overcall then that is probably the reason. You should be getting your own back by playing pre-emptive jump raises as well.

The only difficulty in all this is what do you do with a genuine invitational raise to the three level? The answer in this case is that you cuebid the opponents' suit (2NT is still used as a natural call after an overcall). So both:

    1♡   1♠   2♠   and   1♡   2◇   3◇

would show a sound raise to at least 3♡. This is entirely sensible since you do not need a cuebid of the opponents' overcall suit for any other meaning.

I am assuming here that you play negative doubles. If you do not then you should really give them a chance by having a go at them. When a player of the calibre of Zia Mahmood, who is not noted for being over enamoured of system, says that 'Bridge is not playable without negative doubles', then you ought to give some credence to this. Anyway, assuming that you are playing negative doubles, there is no hand that needs to cuebid the opponents' suit. About the worst hand is a game forcing balanced hand but that can start with a negative double happily enough. Even if you are insistent that a negative double must promise any unbid majors, a strong balanced hand can usually survive this lie. If you cannot stomach that, you can invent a suit to be going on with. No, the cuebid is redundant and hence you can use it to show a good raise in opener's suit. Thus, you can play weak jump raises of opener's suit in competition at effectively no cost at all. It is a win win situation. You get to mess up the opponents' bidding at no cost to your own. I rarely recommend that you should definitely take up a particular method since I am always of the view that it is part of individual preference and partnership philosophy to decide on methods. Here though I am going to recommend it as I see no downside. As I said it is a win-win situation.

Moreover it does not have to stop there. It takes a bit more effort as there is more to consider but many pairs also now play jump raises of responder's suit as pre-emptive in competition. Thus in sequences such as:

1♣	Pass	1♡	2◇
??			

or:

1◇	Pass	1♠	2♡
??			

both 3♡ in the first sequence and 3♠ in the second sequence are regarded as pre-emptive. Again the cuebid (3◇ in the first sequence and 3♡ in the second sequence) shows the good raise in partner's suit. I say it is a little more complicated this time since there are some hands that opener has a problem showing without a cuebid available. In particular opener has a problem showing strong balanced hands without a stop in the opponents' suit and game-forcing one-suited hands. Thus you do need some methods and many expert pairs play either double or 2NT or both as conventional here. The sequences need some effort and system but it is still worth considering playing these kind of pre-emptive raises as well.

Why wait for competition? You can make pre-emptive raises before the opposition have bid at all – a genuine pre-emptive strike. A number of pairs now play all jump raises of opener's suit such as:

1♡	Pass	3♡

as pre-emptive. Clearly this has advantages and can give horrible problems to fourth in hand. They are no longer able to bid at the three level below your suit and may be forced to bid at the three level above your suit when they would be much more comfortable with a two level overcall. Sometimes they pass and miss an easy game, sometimes they bid and partner picks them off for a penalty. Their partner can never tell how good a hand they have; sometimes they pass and miss a game, sometimes they bid a no play one. There is no doubt this is a good idea but again you need to have something to do with a good raise to the three level. Many pairs now play a relatively low-level conventional bid as promising four card support for partner, the most common treatment being to use 2NT. The problem of good raises to the three level can then be solved by including them in this artificial raise. Pre-emptive jumps without competition are not really playable without some sort of gadget like this.

Moving on, how about this hand:

♠ xx
♡ AQJxxx
◊ Axx
♣ xx

You open 1♡ and partner raises you to 2♡. What now? Well, pass of course. You have no chance of making game, so why jeopardise your plus score?

Pass is absolutely bonkers! What is going on in this auction? You have an 11 count and partner has raised 1♡ to 2♡ so will have, say, an average of a 7 count. So you have less than half the pack between you and at least nine, possibly ten, hearts. Whatever you can make, one thing is certain and that is the opponents can make more than you can. Heaven alone knows what planet the opposition have been on up until now but surely if you pass LHO will return to earth and bid something. They must have the world's most obvious protection. So you are likely to give the opponents an easy entry to a making part-score. Worse still they might arrive firmly back on earth and bid a cold game. And all because you were lazy and/or greedy. You should never pass 2♡. You should bid 3♡ as a pre-emptive manoeuvre. Sure you might not make 3♡, but if you cannot then the opponents can easily make at least a partscore and you will still show a profit.

Notice that I am suggesting quite clearly that 3♡ is pre-emptive. It is not any sort of a game try. Generally all raises of a suit partner has supported should be regarded as pre-emptive, having no constructive overtones at all. It helps to keep the opponents out and loses nothing as there are plenty of game tries available; in this case all the other suits and 2NT as well. That should be enough for anybody.

So much for supporting partner, provided you are prepared to define your bidding accordingly you can still pre-empt in competitive auctions without support for the opening bidder. For example, how do you play the sequence:

1♡   1♠   3◊

or the sequence:

1◊   Dble   2♠?

My guess is that unless you have discussed it you will say that it is a force to game with that suit just as if there was no intervention. Do you think this is sensible? Think about when was the last time you had a genuine force to game after an opening bid and a bid from RHO? A year ago? Two years ago? It hardly ever happens. For that reason many pairs are now playing something with a higher frequency. One possibility is to play these bids as weak (weak here defined as whatever one of your weak twos might look like) and hence you are pre-empting the opposition again. So an ideal hand for 3◇ in the first sequence might be:

♠ xx
♡ xx
◇ KQJxxx
♣ xxx

The other common treatment is to treat them as fit jumps. That is they promise a five card suit and four card support for opener, together with enough values to bid to at least three of opener's suit. This method is much more designed to help our side's constructive bidding than pre-empt the opposition's bidding. I do not think it particularly important how you play these sequences but it is worth examining how often you are using your current methods. It is pointless playing these kind of jump shifts as game forces if you never pick them up!

The Opposition Open the Bidding

If more and more sequences after we open the bidding are being played as pre-emptive, this is nothing compared to what is happening after an overcall. A few years ago overcalls, and particularly two level overcalls, showed six card suits and the earth. Then players started to notice that more and more pairs could bid to a sensible contract if they were left to their own devices. So gradually overcalling standards came down and down and raises of overcalls became lighter and lighter. The more you can make the opponents guess the more likely they are to guess wrong.

The basis premise with raising overcalls is the same as with raising opening bids. That is all direct raises are pre-emptive and good raises go through a cuebid of the opponents' suit. What is a good raise or a pre-emptive raise in this case is very much dependent on your precise overcalling style. The lighter your overcalls, the more you need for a good raise.

Let's look at some examples. You hold:

♠ Kxx
♡ xxx
◇ xx
♣ Qxxxx

and the auction goes:

| 1♡ | 1♠ | 2♡ | ? |

This is a clear-cut 2♠ call. You cannot allow your spade support to be kept out of the auction. Partner may not be able to bid again and it is entirely possible that both sides can make two of a major. Indeed Larry Cohen would say that both sides must (well more or less) make two of a major because that is the *Law*. Even if partner was going to bid again your LHO may have been listening to me earlier and bid 3♡ pre-emptively if you pass. Now neither you nor partner will be able to get back into the auction. Bid 2♠ and get your support into the auction. Similarly after:

| 1♡ | 1♠ | Pass | ? |

you must bid 2♠. It is incredibly naive to believe that you are going to be allowed to play in the nice safe contract of 1♠. LHO is never going to pass out 1♠ when you have such a weak hand and such good support for partner. If you pass you allow LHO easy entry at the two level and, you may never be able to show your support. Bid 2♠ and you force the opposition to compete at the three level and you have got your support in. Again we have a win-win situation.

Similarly a pre-emptive raise to 3♠ (some might consider 4♠ at Green though that seems a little excessive to me) is routine on:

♠ Kxxx
♡ xx
◇ xx
♣ Qxxxx

after any of the following sequences:

| 1♡ | 1♠ | 2♡ | ?? |

or:

| 1♡ | 1♠ | Dble | ?? |

or:

| 1♡ | 1♠ | Pass | ?? |

Particularly in the last sequence do not be seduced by RHO's pass. So they have not got very much, this just means that LHO has even more. You are never going to be allowed to play 1♠ or even 2♠. You are going to be pushed to 3♠ anyway, so take the entire three level away from the opposition quickly with an immediate pre-emptive 3♠.

If you have a hand good enough for a sound raise you can cuebid to show this. So for example, with:

♠ Kxx
♡ xxx
◇ AQxx
♣ Qxx

after:

1♡   1♠   Pass   ?

we would bid 2♡ and pass 2♠ if that is all partner can do (unless you are playing a very sound overcalling style in which case you might consider raising to 3♠). With a better hand, say the ♣A rather than the ♣Q, we would cuebid and then raise 2♠ to 3♠ to show a good raise to 3♠.

Finally, how do you play your jump overcalls of the opponents opening bid? That is calls such as:

1♡   3◇   or   1◇   2♠

If your answer is strong, non-forcing then you are a dying breed. In Britain intermediate jump overcalls are quite common but in most of the rest of the world weak jump overcalls are considered routine. That is, all jumps after the opponents open are weak, just how weak depending on all the usual factors such as vulnerability, position at the table, partnership philosophy, how many imps down you are, etc. Pre-emptive jumps can as usual cause some real headaches for the opposition by removing some, on occasions vital, bidding room. It is not essential to play jump overcalls to show any other hand strength since intermediate hands can make a simple overcall and strong hands can double and then bid the suit (or also just make a simple overcall if you are a modernist).

Well, that's about it. That is a quick canter through the main areas of pre-emptive bidding in competition. As you can see enormous numbers of sequences, including effectively all raises, are now being defined as pre-emptive by the cognoscenti. So if you find that the opposition are always